To Linda

ALL AMERICAN LETTERS HOME

Written by Private First Class
Earl Gene Thurman

Andrew Vincent Garner

"Thank you for your support"

Andy

A V Garner
2024

ISBN 978-1-7385125-0-8

Acknowledgments:

To my family: Mum and Dad, Ronnie, and Margaret Garner; my daughter, Shannen Featherstone, who gave me moral support and ideas, my son, Toby Garner, for his guidance in researching the 82nd Airbourne; my son-in-law, Callum Featherstone, keen to see me complete this project; Ann Marie Brown for her generosity, without it, this book would never have been; my loving partner who gave the idea and encouraged me throughout, Lex Duncan; Phil Samponaro, historical researcher and friend; Rob Morris, an inspirational author and friend; the East Texas Historical Association, Gary Pinkerton, Dave and Libby Hill Nelson, Tiffany Wright Smith County Historical Society for support with research; Martin Chapman for encouragement; Mike Ager for his friendship, support, and guidance; Thomas Arnold for his support; Jon Jordan for his advice; Sandra Lawrence, author and friend for the valued advice. Tim Pitts, author and freelance photojournalist, Paul O'Donnell, author, and poet:
Dianne Ingram for her enthusiastic encouragement: Finally, Sven Dautzenberg a modern-day veteran in his own right, whose support in forthcoming projects has been immense.

82nd Airborne a brief history:

The 82nd Airborne was formed in 1917, as America entered the First World War, serving with distinction on the Western Front. The original formation of the division involved members joining from all the 48 states of America gaining the nickname "All-American", hence the very recognisable shoulder patch featuring AA as its main symbol, after the WW1 the division was deactivated in 1919.
During the Second World War, the Division reactivated in 1942, becoming the first airborne division in the history of the U.S. Army. It consisted of the 505th Parachute Infantry Regiment (505th PIR) 504th PIR and the 325th Glider infantry Regiment, along with other Regiments and Battalions.

The first combat parachute assaults took place in 1943 with the 505th Parachute Infantry Regiment spearheading the Allied invasion of Sicily and Salemo. After fighting in Italy, they took part in operation OVERLORD, the allied assault of Normandy in June 1944 with 12,000 Parachute and glider troops where they fought for 33 days without relief or replacements. Later in the same year they jumped into Holland as part of Operation MARKET GARDEN, the main objectives to capture and hold the key bridges at Grave and Nijmegen. Following this, the division took part in ground assaults with the last major German offensive in December 1944, the Battle of the Bulge, before pushing towards the river Rhine and into Germany. Towards the end of the Second World War, the 82nd Airborne liberated a work camp at Wobbelin, Germany and received the unconditional surrender of over 146,000 soldiers of the 21st German Army.
These pioneering paratroopers "Stood up, hooked up" jumping from C-47 transport planes or the Waco CG-4 gliders, receiving 9,073 battle casualties, 1,619 killed in action, with four men receiving the Medal of Honour, the United States Armed Forces highest award for acts of valour.

Private John R. Towle, Private First-Class Charles N. Deglopper, Private Joe Gandara were all awarded posthumously, with Joe Gandara being awarded the medal of honor by President Barrack Obama in 2014 after the Defence Authorization Act which called for a review of Jewish and Hispanic American veterans who served in

World War 2, the Korean War, and the Vietnam War. The final medal of honor was awarded to First Sergeant Leonard A. Funk Jr. for his actions of January 29th, 1945. The 82nd division would make the most American combat jumps during the Second World War.

Mail Call:

Throughout the Second World War, letters to those in the service, especially those overseas, helped maintain morale. Hearing the words called out "MAIL CALL" followed by your name as you had received a letter, or a parcel was an uplifting experience, even during the toughest of times. Craving news from home was a prize any service personnel treasured. For a moment, the letters became an escape from reality. Various forms of mail were dispatched, the amount posted in 1945 going back and forth across the Atlantic and Pacific, from the Army postal service, the majority by the Naval postal service was estimated at around eleven billion letters. Regular handwritten letters were the best to receive, especially if sent via air mail. This proved to be one of the faster services although it could take over a month to reach an individual sometimes longer, the quality was much better than the V-mail.

The introduction of the V-mail or "Victory mail" in 1942, was based on the British Airgraph from the 1930's, it became a way in which to reduce the size of the vast amount of mail sent by ship, allowing more space for important supplies. It was claimed that 1-600 letters could weigh 50 pounds, while the V-mail for the same number of letters would be 5 ounces. This meant 37 mail bags that would carry 150,000 one-page letters could be reduced to one mail sack. V-mails were written on a sheet 7 inches by 9 1/8 inches, these would be censored before being photographed to a thumb-nail size then stored as a negative on microfilm. When the microfilm reached its destination, the letters would be printed to a size of 4 1/2 inches by 5 ¼ inches. The trouble with the V-mails when they were developed proved they could be extremely difficult to read, if at all. Another limitation to the V-mail was the amount that could be written compared to a normal letter.

Corporal Eugene S. Howland 635th Tank Destroyer Battalion wrote on March 16th, 1944, from England to the U.S.A.

"Received your most welcome letter that you mailed on the 18th Feb two days ago, so it took 25 days to make the trip I also received one from mother the same day that had been on the way four days longer. Both of them were straight free mail, on Sat. March.11th I received one from mother that was air mail & it took just twelve days, so their mail is much faster so far. Received my first V mail letter today from Bernice and it took 14 days, the V mail is faster than the straight mail but you sure can't write much on it, isn't so bad for us to use it for we don't have much to write about or what we can write about, but we always like to get big letters here. Had one air mail letter from Long Beach Calif. in nine days."

Preface:

Paratrooper Private First Class, Earl Gene Thurman.

Earl Gene Thurman, born 5th January 1924, and was raised in East Point, Georgia, USA, a town originally named for being the end of the line for a railroad terminus in 1870. The town originally housed around 12 families, but by 1940 the population had grown to 12,500. Earl attended Russell High School, while also working as a retail grocery clerk aged 16, earning $2.50 per month, he would eventually graduate from Emory University. Later he was employed by the Westinghouse Electric Company before his draft came through to join the military on June 30th, 1942.

The Westinghouse Electric Company began life as one of the original companies to build the American Electric infrastructure. During the period Earl was employed in the early 1940s, the company was involved in the manufacture of radar defence systems, jet engines and even making liners for M1 helmets. The standard helmet as worn by all branches of military service, the liners would make the helmet more comfortable to wear and could be worn without the steel outer, often used to hold water to wash with while in the field.

The following letters, V-mails, and postcards were written, not by my hand, but by the hand of the late Private First-Class Earl G. Thurman, he served with the 82nd Airborne as a replacement G.I. in the Second World War. Age has muddled some, with letters approaching 80 years old; they have overall stood the test of time, yellowing in some places torn and holed in others, but wherever possible each letter has been carefully copied exactly including the punctuation. Minimal author's discretion has been used, but only when the print was unreadable or damaged.

The letters tell of a young Southern American serviceman, his story, his words, writing home to loved ones. You read of his time in basic training, the joys of exploring and visiting new places in the U.S.A as he travels to various Army camps. Then to England where Earl is struck by the beauty of the English countryside, the people, even the local dialects. Next, into the thick of battle as he parachutes into Holland during operation Market Garden.

Operation Market Garden was the largest Allied airborne operation in history, its aim was to secure the bridges over the rivers Maas, Waal, and Rhine in the Netherlands to outflank the heavy German defences of the Siegfried Line and to ensure a swift advance toward Berlin. Although Operation Market Garden was ultimately a failure, its objectives were not achieved because of the unforeseen strength of the German fighting force. The sheer determination and courage shown by the Allied airborne troops, and the units that assisted them, made it one of the Second World War's most famous battles.

Later in the conflict, a telegram home informs the Thurman family that Earl has been wounded in action. This unveils a unique history trail, as letters, hospital cards, and memorabilia give the reader a perspective of an American wounded serviceman directly from his point of view using his own collection of memorabilia. Earl wrote home regularly to his mother, Launette Glass Thurman, his father, Earl Van Dorn Thurman, Daddy, and his sister Nell. His story starts from basic training and the excitement of visiting unfamiliar places both home and overseas. Revealed is the importance of contact, hearing from loved ones, the frustration of not receiving a letter or a parcel, and the censorship limitations. Army life can be dull, this becomes obvious, some letters tend to repeat a similar message time and time again. With this collection of ephemera came priceless photos, booklets, and interesting documents, which I have to the best of my knowledge, included in date order and relevance.

Researching Earl has been a revelation; a case of how one door opens another, the power of social media, the World Wide Web, even a very well-known online auction site. In one of Earl's letters there is a very brief mention of a parcel received by Miss Parr from Russell, an educated guess led me to discern that Russell was a High School in East Point, Georgia, Earl's hometown. A quick search on an auction site for school yearbooks from the Russell High School dating from the early 1940s revealed three for sale. A message was sent to the sellers, in the hope they could flick through the yearbooks looking for a photograph or evidence of Earl or Miss Parr. It was meant to be as the first seller took the time to look through a 1940 Russell High School book. There was nothing on Earl, but a photo of Miss Parr which led to a conversation about why an Englishman was enquiring about two American citizens. Dave Nelson the seller, was informed of my reason for purchase, he immediately reduced the price on the yearbook, and took an interest in my search for Earl's story. With his help my search for information widened and opened the story immensely. With the discovery of historical sites, especially the "East Texas Historical Association" and Gary Pinkerton, who researched newspaper articles on my behalf, the conclusion will shock.

Take a deep breath…

Sit back…

Imagine hearing Gene's Southern accent in your mind...

Read his words, turn back the clock…

As you listen to a young man at war…

1943

Pvt. Earl Gene Thurman

Enlisted in February 1943, aged twenty.

Pictured are Earl's garrison caps or side caps as possibly seen worn in the previous photograph, he would have purchased these privately from the PX "Post Exchange", a specific Army retail store that sells goods to military personnel. Private purchase caps were preferred by many to the issued type as they had a smarter look and were better fitting.

The piping on the cap was colour coded depending on the service you were attached to or your rank. Light blue piping pictured on Earl's caps denoted he was in the US infantry.

Sunday Night
March 21, 1943

Dear Daddy

Received your letter this morning and surely was glad to hear from you. Sorry you have had more trouble with your knee, as mother wrote. Hope it isn't bothering you now.

Army life is proving to be alright, I like it more as I become familiar with it. Today has really been a day of rest with me, or at least I hadn't had any orders to obey, but I ran the obstacle course this morning and rambled in the woods quite a bit this afternoon, alone of course, and it a wonder I didn't get lost. Yesterday I took a three-hour test for Officers Training School. Of course that doesn't mean I'll become an officer by a long ways. And speaking of officers, we have a nice bunch of commissioned officers and non-commissioned officers. I have met a number of very nice fellows since

I have been here. I am in a new regiment, and there is lots of room for promotion. Each regiment has a heavy weapons company, and I'm in one. That includes heavy machine guns and trench mortars.

A number of new men got week-end passes this week. I was eligible but had to take the test, and was not able to get ~~of~~ out of the fort. I don't know where I would have gone if I had, although there are lots of sights I would like to see with in reasonable distance of the fort.

Well, its almost time for lights out, so I guess I'd better stop. Will write more when I have time.

Love,
Gene

Pvt Earl G. Thurman
Co "D" 324 th Inf. Reg
A.P.O. #44
Fort Louis, Wash (Stato)

Mr. E.r. Thurman
304 n. Cheney St.
East Point, Georgia

Sunday Night

March 21, 1943

Dear Daddy

Received your letter this morning and surely was glad to hear from you. Sorry you have had more trouble with your knee, as mother wrote. Hope it isn't bothering you now.

`Army life is proving to be alright, I like it more as I become familiar with it. Today has really been a day of rest with me, or at least I haven't had any orders to obey, but I ran the obstacle course this morning and rambled in the woods quite a bit this afternoon, alone of course, and its a wonder I didn't get lost. Yesterday I took a three-hour test for officer training school. Of course that doesn't mean I'll become an officer by a long ways. And speaking of officers, we have a nice bunch of commissioned officers and non-commissioned officers. I have met a number of very nice fellows since I have been here. I am in a new regiment, and there is lots of room for promotion. Each regiment has a heavy weapon company and I'm in one. That includes heavy machine guns and trench mortars.

A number of our men got weekend passes this week. I was eligible but had to take the test, and was not able to get out of the fort. I don't know where I would have gone if I had, although there are lots of sights I would like to see with in reasonable distance of the fort.

Well, it's almost time for lights out, so I guess I'd better stop. Will write more when I have time.

Love,
Gene

Pvt Earl G. Thurman
Co "D" 324 th Inf. Reg
A.P.O. #44
Fort Louis, Wash

Mr. E.r. Thurman
304 n. Cheney St.
East Point, Georgia

Sunday A.M. April 4, 1943

Dear Daddy,

Received your letter two or three days ago, but have been so too busy to write many letters. I did, however get around to writing mother, and of course her letters are intended for you also. I think you will find most of my "Army" news in her letter. I believe I mentioned the fact that we have a complete "layout" inspection Saturday morning (every week), at which time we have our own equipment all cleaned and laid out on our bunk for the inspecting officer to look at.

We have to "dress up" and stand by our bunk and attempt to answer any questions he may wish to ask. If the officer isn't satisfied with our equipment it's too bad for us. I also mentioned the fact that all weekend passes had been cancelled, and there were to be none issued this week. What I am getting around to is we had a good inspection, and the ban on passes was lifted, so here I am in Seattle, about fifty miles from camp. I was issued my pass yesterday about two o:clock, and being ready to leave headed straight for the bus depot. There was and estimated ten thousand buying tickets and five thousand who had brought tickets and were waiting on buses. (I did the estimating). I hit things lucky after I once got my ticket and was on the bus by a quarter to three. There is no direct bus line to Seattle from the fort, so we come to Tacoma and changed busses. I really hit it lucky at Tacoma, by getting the first bus out, after I had just time enough to buy my ticket. Up to that time I had been with two more boys from the fort but I was just ahead of them in the line, and the last one on the bus, so I left them at the station, and am now a lone wolf, finding my way around as best I can, I've done very good so far, however as you could easily imagine the problems of finding a place to sleep is a major one, especially late Sat night. I arrived here about six, wandered around a bit, went to an army store and brought a few things I needed., and finally found a nice restaurant, where I got a delicious sirloin steak with French fries, bread and butter, milk, and dessert. They don't give it away though.

By the time I finished I owed the man a dollar and a half but it was really worth it to me. After that, since it was about eight-thirty, I started looking for a room. I walked across the street to a nice looking hotel and asked the clerk if he had any rooms. All he had was a cot in a hallway which had been partitioned off just to accommodate the crowd. Of course that was just what I wanted, for it only cost one dollar and I had expected to sleep in the street somewhere. It is really just what I wanted, kind of small room without a door, but it is private enough. After I got the room I went out and bummed around a bit then came back and went to bed. After a good nights sleep, I arose about nine o'clock and back to the restaurant where I had my breakfast of pancakes and sausage. Then I came back to the room and started writing this letter. After being in camp so long it feels swell to be a human being again. I guess I'll go back to camp early this afternoon, although I don't have to be back until eleven o:clock tonight.

I hope that things at home are swell and you and mother both are feeling well. Give mother my love and I shall remain,

Your Loving son,

Gene

Pvt. Earl Gene Thurman training photo, 1944

Photographs, taken while in training in New Orleans 1944:

French Quarter - N.O.
This is Royale Street -
location of the many
antique shops, and also
of the Hotel Monteleone,
where we stayed one
Night.

French Quarter – N.O. This is Royal Street – location of many antique shops, and also of the Hotel Monteleone, where we stayed one night.

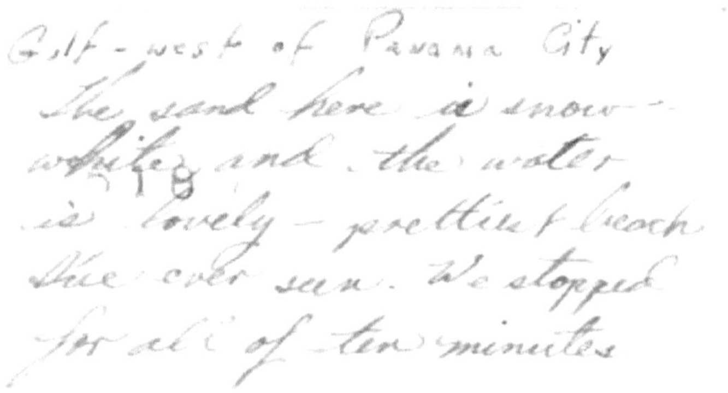
Gulf - west of Panama City
The sand here is snow-
white and the water
18
is lovely - prettiest beach
I've ever seen. We stopped
for all of ten minutes

Gulf– west of Panama City, the sand here is snow white and the water is lovely – prettiest beach I've ever seen.
We stopped for all of ten minutes

Lake Bell Gardens

Lake, Bell Gardens

Lake + Boat house - Bell. Gardens

518

Lake + Boat house – Bell. Gardens

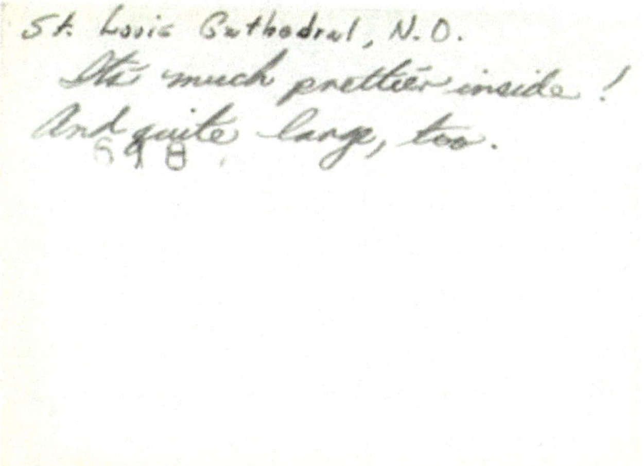
St. Louis Cathedral, N.O.
It's much prettier inside!
And quite large, too.

St. Louis Cathedral, N.O. It's much prettier inside!
And quite large, too.

Amongst the collection were several booklets including this handbook of information for Camp Fannin, Texas. This was designed to inform the new recruits of everything they should know about the training center and its facilities. A copy could also be purchased at five cents from the post exchange to send home to family and friends, to show them about your new life in the Army.

1944

T/5 Earl G. Thurman 34760054
Co "L" 1st P.T.R. C1#120
Fort Benning, Georgia (A.T.A.)

Mr. E.r. Thurman
304 n. Cheney St.
East Point, Georgia

Thursday Night
April 21, 1944

Dear Daddy,

Well, how is everything at home now? I hope you are getting enough to eat or I should say the right things to eat.

I hope I can get home soon to cook you up a good chow or two! Never can tell when I am going to "pop" in.

I feel much better now that four days of my first week, or "A" stage, is over. I only have one more day now, and then Saturday we cross the river and go over to Georgia for my remaining three weeks of jump training, "B","C", & "D" stages.

This week has been mostly physical conditioning, but in "B" stage we have a lot of ' chute packing and harness work. In "C" stage we jump from high towers by a chute and land on our own. They say that is a lot of fun. Then comes good old "D" stage, when we make our five jumps from a real plane. We make four daytime jumps and one at night, which qualify us as paratroopers. Surprisingly enough, the night jump is said to be the easiest, except for the long fifteen mile hike after the jump.

Well hope to see you soon. Have to stop now as the lights are going out.

Gene

Official War Department training film 1943:

"So, you want to be a parachutist. Good that means you have courage, but don't think being brave makes jumping a snitch, you're going to find out theres a lot more to it than making breath taking leaps out of flying transport."

Four weeks of intensive training began with "A" stage physical conditioning ". As quoted "if your middle is flabby, this will turn into armour plate". The trainees learned how to tumble correctly and how to deal with landing shock, while getting back on their feet in the shortest possible time.

Part of "B" stage, trainees worked on training aids that helped them learn the details of the parachute jump, including how to fit a harness. In a model aircraft, "HOOK UP" was taught with the static line. (This line releases the chute by being attached to a line within the aircraft.) As trainees jumped, the line unwound as they fell. When the distance of 15 feet was reached, the parachute was deployed by pulling open the pack. Once they had mastered jumping from the aircraft exit in 8 seconds, their courage was tested as they used towers to practice the correct body positioning as they exited, turning left as they jumped to face the tail of the airplane while attached to a zip wire. During this stage they learned the famous "BATTLE CALL", the three second count. "One thousand", "Two thousand", "Three thousand". If they hadn't felt the shock release of the main canopy at this time, they then had to pull the reserve chute.

"C" stage aimed to get trainees accustomed to being under a canopy at height. Using a high tower, they were drawn up to its limit then released while still being attached to a line, this descent was a lot quicker than the real parachute fall. Part two of the "C" stage training, involved another decent from the highest towers, the trainees were first told to check the wind direction by dropping a piece of paper, then the canopy was released un-attached. Trainees had then completed their first solo jump on landing. Detachment of the harness was learnt along with how to spill their canopy should it fill with air, this could drag them uncontrollably along the surface, causing all sorts of problem if not sorted quickly.

"D" stage, the fourth and final week of training, trainees had to make five solo parachute jumps from an aircraft. Upon completion, they became a member of an elite airborne parachute force.

Postcard sent from Fort Benning
June 8, 1944

T/5 Earl G. Thurman
Btry "L" 8th Bn 2nd P.T.R.
Ft. Benning, Ga (A.T.A.)

Mrs E.V. Thurman
304 N. Cheney St.
East Point, Ga

Wednesday A.M.

Dear Mother,

Well I still don't know what I'm going to do here, nor how long I will stay. I don't believe it will be so long, however. Yesterday we turned in our extra clothing and were issued a lot of new clothing. I don't know what we will do for the rest of the week, or whether I'll be home for the week-end, week. By the time you get this card I may have wired for money, for I don't have enough money to get home. I'll write if I hear any news.

Love,
Gene

Postcard sent to Earl's mother, June 8th, 1944.

T/5 Earl G. Thurman
Btry "L" 8th Bn. 2nd P.T.R.
Ft. Benning, Ga. (A.I.S.)

Free

POST CARD

FORT BENNING, GA.
JUN 8
1944

Mrs. E. V. Thurman
304 N. Cheney St.
East Point, Ga.

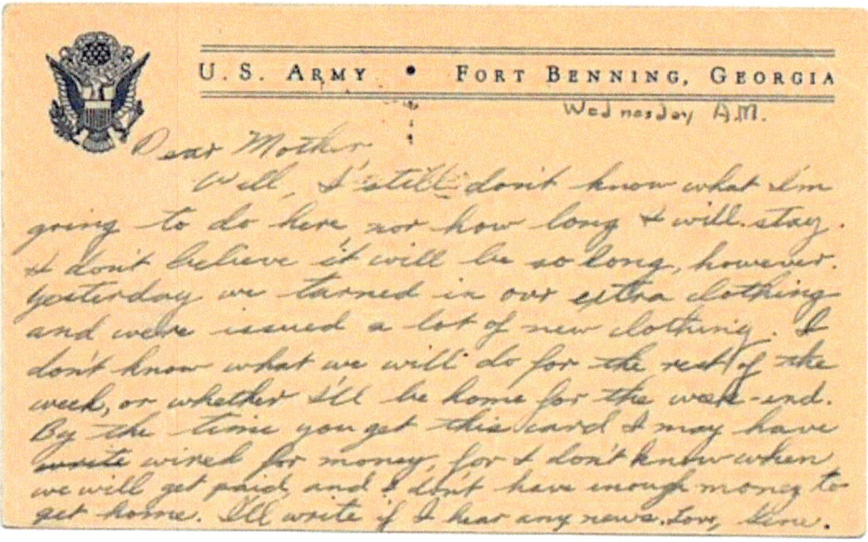
U. S. ARMY • FORT BENNING, GEORGIA

Wednesday A.M.

Dear Mother,

Well, I still don't know what I'm going to do here nor how long I will stay. I don't believe it will be so long, however. Yesterday we turned in our extra clothing and were issued a lot of new clothing. I don't know what we will do for the rest of the week, or whether I'll be home for the week-end. By the time you get this card I may have ~~wrote~~ wired for money for I don't know when we will get paid, and I don't have enough money to get home. I'll write if I hear any news. Love, Gene.

Postcard sent from Fort Benning
June 21, 1944

Pvt. Earl G. Thurman
Co "D" 6th Bn 2nd P.T.R.
Ft. Benning, Ga.

Miss Nell Thurman
304 N. Cheney St.
East Point, Ga

Dear Nell,

I don't need to tell you what my plans for the immediate future are, for I've written Mother about them. I do want you to write me your future New York address, for I may be able to see you before I go across, that is, If I go do it. Meade I certainly do hope I go there. I may even get to see Lenie, but I'm not making plans yet. I'll wait until I get there. I write again soon.

Be sweet, love,

Gene

Postcard sent from Fort Benning
June 21, 1944

Pvt. Earl G. Thurman
Co "D" 6th Bn 2nd PTR
Ft. Benning, Ga

Mrs E.V. Thurman
304 N. Cheney St.
East Point, Ga

Tuesday P.M.

Dear Mother,

I wrote you this morning, and told you about shipping out, and now I am almost sure that I was right. This afternoon we went over and had all our clothes taken up and new ones issued. We left our new clothes at the supply building and only have one suit and our toilet articles with us now. Don't worry about the suit at home – I don't need it.

I'll write again soon.

Love,

Gene

Notice of change of address, June 27th, 1944.

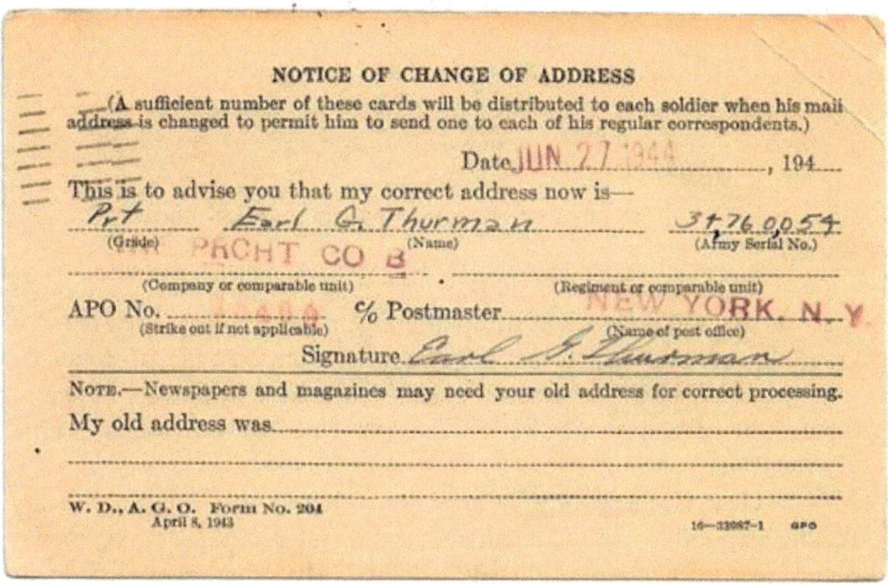

NOTICE OF CHANGE OF ADDRESS

(A sufficient number of these cards will be distributed to each soldier when his mail address is changed to permit him to send one to each of his regular correspondents.)

Date JUN 27 1944, 194

This is to advise you that my correct address now is—

Pvt (Grade) Earl G. Thurman (Name) 37760054 (Army Serial No.)

PRCHT CO B (Company or comparable unit) (Regiment or comparable unit)

APO No. (Strike out if not applicable) % Postmaster NEW YORK, N. Y. (Name of post office)

Signature Earl G. Thurman

Note.—Newspapers and magazines may need your old address for correct processing.

My old address was

W. D., A. G. O. Form No. 204
April 8, 1943

16—33087-1 GPO

Service Club
Fort George G. Meade
Maryland

Tuesday P.M.
June 27, 1944

Dear Mother,

Just a short note to let you, Nell and Daddy know what I'm doing.

I spent most of yesterday getting my clothes and equipment ready to go, and have spent some of today in like manner. We are most certainly going to ship sometime this afternoon. I don't know exactly when, I don't know where we're going, nor how long we will stay. I have hope of going to N.Y. or some place nearby, but I don't know yet.

How is everybody getting along these days? I hope you are feeling as good as you were when I left, if not better. Just take it easy! I know you find that very hard to do though. When does Nell leave New York? I don't know whether she will be there this weekend or not, but maybe I will hear from you before then.

I don't know whether I will need that money or not, but when you get it please send in on. I don't want to get caught "broke" on my last week or two in the states! I'll write again as soon as I arrive at any new address.

Love to all,
Gene

SERVICE CLUB

UNITED STATES ARMY

Friday Night
June 30, 1944

Dear Mother,

I still haven't heard from home since I left Fort Benning, but I hope everything is alright with you and Daddy. Maybe "no news is good news". I guess by now Nell has gone to New York, and I hope she likes it there and does fine.

I don't think I will get to see her for we are not getting any passes now. We are just too busy I guess, and getting busier all the time. I may not have a chance to write again while I'm in the States, but please don't worry if you don't hear for quite a while. I will be alright, and I will write just as soon as I can.

I like the fellows here much better than any I've seen since I've been in the "Troopers". I guess they are somewhat more serious than they have been before. I am really glad I'm in now and I think I will have a lot of fun, along with the rest, even after we get across. There is never a dull moment here, and that is nice when you can't be home any. And you don't have a chance to get home any.

There is little more I can say, although I wish I could write more. This is certainty a short letter.

By the way, if you should want to send me something, you may send an eight ounce package anytime, and a five pound package on my request. However, I don't know that I will need anything. We are still able to get our necessities even "over there".

Give my love to all, and just remember to be calm about me. I'll write as soon as I can.

Lots of love,

Gene

Original copy of previous letter, likely the last one written by Earl before embarking to England.

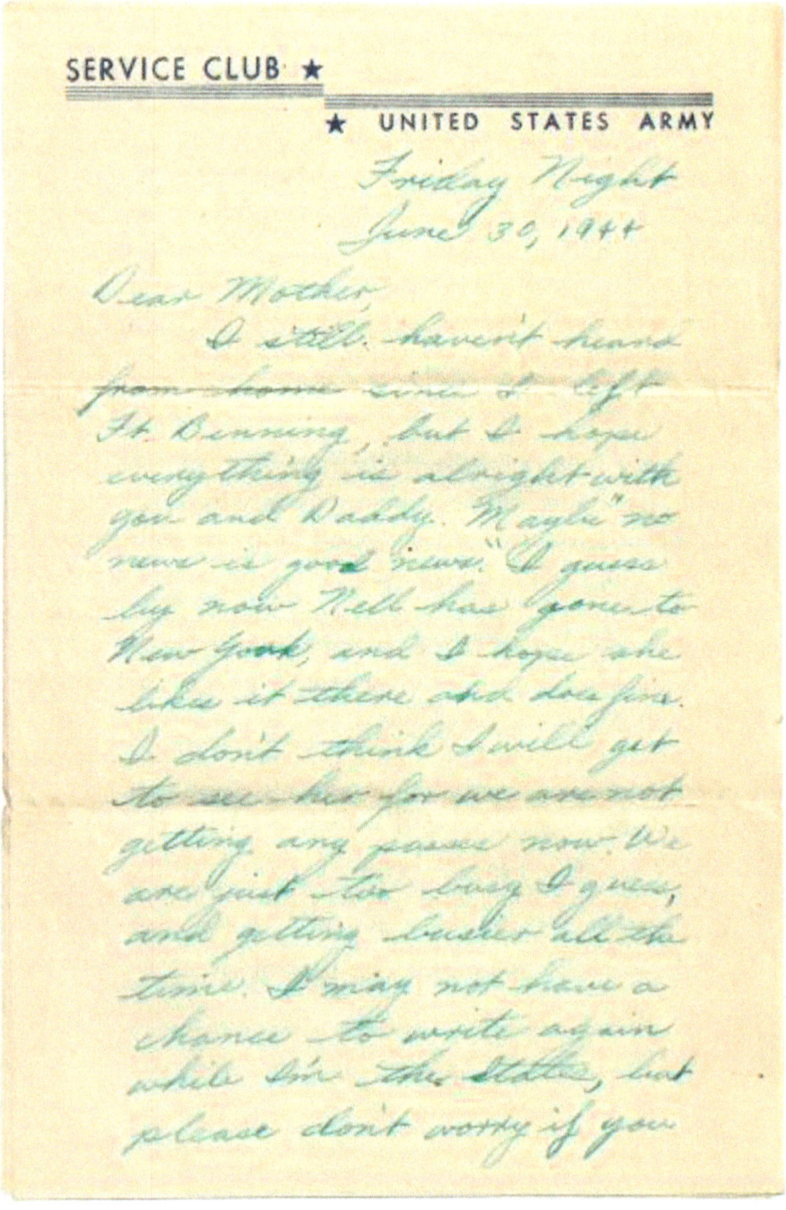

SERVICE CLUB ★

★ UNITED STATES ARMY

Friday Night
June 30, 1944

Dear Mother,

I still haven't heard from home since I left Ft. Benning, but I hope everything is alright with you and Daddy. Maybe "no news is good news." I guess by now Nell has gone to New York, and I hope she likes it there and does fine. I don't think I will get to see her for we are not getting any passes now. We are just too busy I guess, and getting busier all the time. I may not have a chance to write again while in the States, but please don't worry if you

ENGLAND

“P.S. I’m now in England!”

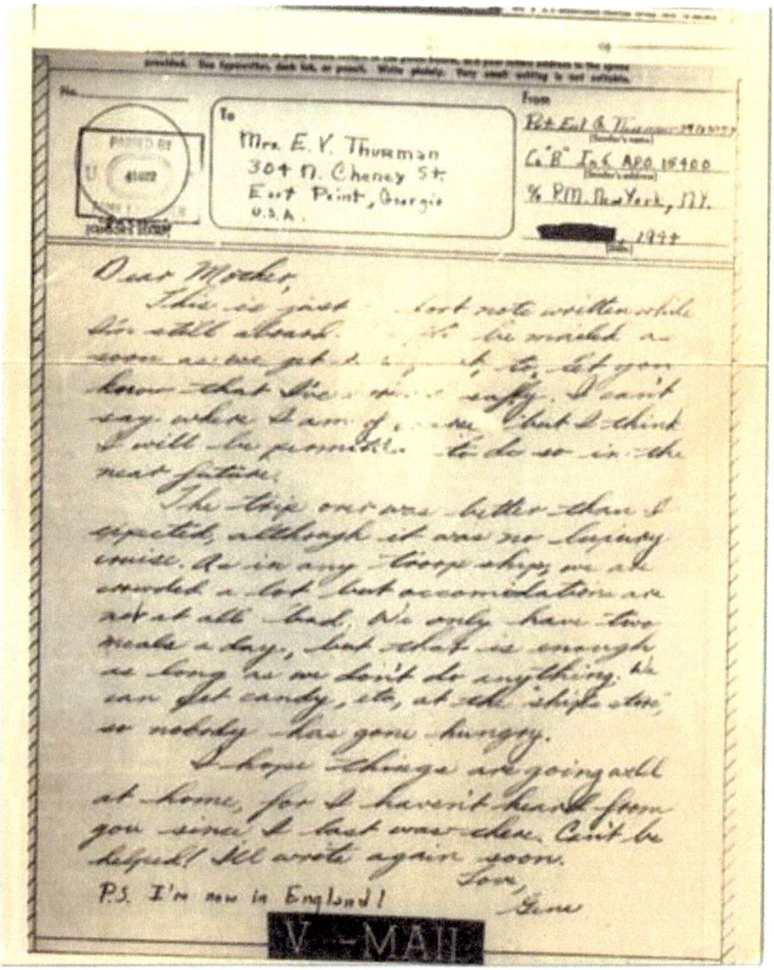

To
Mrs. E. V. Thurman
304 N. Cheney St.
East Point, Georgia
U.S.A.

From
Pvt. Earl G. Thurman [illegible]
Co. "B" Inf. APO 15400
% P.M. New York, N.Y.
[redacted], 1944

Dear Mother,

This is just [illegible] short note written while I'm still aboard. [illegible] be mailed as soon as we get [illegible] to let you know that I've [illegible] safely. I can't say where I am of [illegible] but I think I will be permitted to do so in the near future.

The trip over was better than I expected, although it was no luxury cruise. As in any troop ship, we are crowded a lot but accomodations are not at all bad. We only have two meals a day, but that is enough as long as we don't do anything. We can get candy, etc. at the "ship's store," so nobody has gone hungry.

I hope things are going well at home, for I haven't heard from you since I last was there. Can't be helped! I'll write again soon.

Love,
Gene

P.S. I'm now in England!

V-MAIL

Mrs. E.V. Thurman
304 N. Cheney St.
East Point, Georgia
U.S.A

Pvt. Earl G Thurman 34766054
Co "B" Inf A.P.O. 15400
c/o P.M. New York, N.Y.

Date Censored (Erased) 1944

Dear Mother,

This is just a short note written while I'm still aboard. I'm to be mobilized as soon as we get the green light, just to let you know that I've arrived safely. I can't say where I am of course but I think I will be permitted to do so in the near future.

The trip over was better than I expected, although it was no luxury cruise. As in any troop ship, we are crowded a lot but accommodations are not at all bad. We only have two meals a day, but that is enough as long as we don't do anything. We can get candy, etc, at the "ships store", so nobody has gone hungry. I hope things are going well at home, for I haven't heard from you since I last was there. Can't be helped!

I'll write again soon,

Gene

P.s I'm now in England!

Earl would have left America and embarked on a troop ship at New York, arriving at Liverpool, England, quite possibly on the Queen Elizabeth or Queen Mary, both luxury liners were converted to troop ships. These powerful ships could run a straight route to their destination outrunning the dreaded U-boat (German submarine) Wolfpacks. Slower troop ships would zig-zag their way across the ocean in the hope of avoiding detection with destroyer and air cover protection. The German U-boat Wolfpacks were the scourge of the ocean in the early part of the war, sinking many allied merchant ships, they would hunt ships in groups in a similar manner to a pack of wolves.

Mrs. E.V. Thurman
304 N. Cheney St.
East Point, Georgia

Pvt. Earl G. Thurman
34760054
Co "B" Inf. A.P.O. 15400
c/o PM New York.

July 12th, 1944

Dear Mother,

Well, by now I guess you know that I'm in jolly old England, So today I will try to tell you what I think it's like.

I have been constantly impressed by the neatness and orderliness of everything, both in the city and country. I am very conveniently located at a nice city and have had the opportunity to see parts of it.

I like both the city and it's people, and the English seem to be quite cheerful and cordial, despite the war and its effect on England. Things here are much the same as in America, although on a some what smaller scale. The place at which I am staying is very nice and the food is good. Yes I'm quite happy to be here as long as I can't be home. I am having experiences I would never had as a civilian. I hope you get this letter and the other one (Page Two) at the same time!

The only two things here that can be confusing are the difference in accents and in the money system. So far, however I've had no trouble with either and after a few more passes and chances to associate with the English I'm sure I'll be right at "home"!

I received you letter with the money at noon yesterday, and thank you very much. I was certainly glad to get some news from home. I am happy to know things are fine. I know corresponding will be more difficult and more brief on my part now, but I think I will be able to write at least twice a week. That will be enough to say and all I can tell after the "new" wears off. Don't think I will need more money. We can't spend much here anyway.

I guess this about completes my news for today. Mother please don't worry about me. Things are not half as bad as you think, not even in combat, and I won't be there for a while yet. Hope to hear from you soon.

Love to you & Daddy,

Gene

Mrs. E. V. Thurman
304 N. Cheney St
East Point, Georgia

Pvt. Earl G. Thurman
34760054
Co "E" 505th Prcht Inf. APO 469
c/o P.M. New York, N.Y.

July 22nd, 1944

Dear Mother,

Well I have nothing new to write, but I know you like to hear from me anyway. I guess my letters have been rather infrequent since I left the U.S. but it can't be helped. I haven't heard from you recently either but I have no need to cause to worry about things at home. I just hope that things are fine, and don't let it bother you when you don't hear I realize it can't be helped.

The discipline is going to be much more rigid here than it has been at other places, but it is for our own good, and we will be better off once we get in the swing of things. There is no such thing as a "weekend pass" around here, nor in any part of England. I guess they think no one has any Special business that requires that long to transact of course with transportation the way it is, the men wouldn't go anywhere without tying up transportation facilities. I would like to see more of England, but I may have the chance before I get away from it.

Yesterday our commanding officer decided the grass was getting to high, so we got down on our hands & knees and pulled it up with our hands. It was quite a job, and seemed rather useless to me. This is still the U.S. Army I guess.

I believe this is all I can say anyway just now. Here's hoping you and Daddy are fine.

Lots of love,
Gene

Mrs. E. V. Thurman
304 N. Cheney St
East Point, Georgia

Pvt Earl G. Thurman
A.S.N. 34760054
Co "E" 505 Prcht Inf APO 469
c/o PM New York N.Y.

July 24th, 1944

Dear Mother,

Well I received two letters from you today, one dated July 7th the other the 5th, and I really enjoyed them. As soon as our mail once starts going straight through the service will be much better I'm sure. I now have my permanent A.P.O. number and will not be moving around again soon. I still haven't been assigned to a regular company, but I think it will be tomorrow.

Things are still going along fine, the food here is really good. I come away from the mess hall full after every meal. That is something that never happens in the "States".

We don't have any milk, but other things make up for it. Transportation here in England isn't as good as that back home, so I've solved the problem by purchasing a "bike" It is one of the English type, very light, and will be ideal for going to the nearby towns in the evenings. If I tire of it I can always sell it for at least the cost, probably more. I think I will enjoy it however.

There are a few things that I am going to need, but I will wait until I think of more before I send a bit. The reality of course, that nothing is urgent – just convenience that we can't get here. Hope you and Daddy are fine.

Lots of love,
Gene

Postal date July 24th, 1944

Mrs E.V. Thurman
304 N. Cheney St
East Point

Pvt. Earl G. Thurman
34260054
Co. "B" Prcht. Inf.
A.P.O. 15900

Dear Mother

Well, how is everything at home? Going well, I hope. Nothing special is happening with me. I am still at the same place and am still having a nice time, as far as army life goes. The weather is pleasant, and not hot, as it is at home. As you can guess I am rather busy and don't have much time for writing. I guess it will be that way as long as I'm over here, but there is a little I can say it doesn't matter much.

From the news, the war in Europe is going quite well, and let's hope its over soon and we can all come home! I'll write again soon and I do hope I have something to say next time.

Lots of love,

Gene

Mrs E.V. Thurman
304 N. Cheney St.
East Point, Georgia

Pvt. Earl G. Thurman
A.S.N. 34760054
Co "G" 505 Prcht. Inf. A.P.O. 469
c/o P.M. New York, N.Y.

July 26th, 1944

Dear Mother

Well I have at last been assigned to my permanent company, and am very glad to be in this one. I've only been here two days, but the men seem to be very nice. Best ones I've seen since I've been in the army.

Most of them have been through the invasion of Sicily, Italy, as well as France. They tell some exciting tales, but they don't bragg about the things they've done. Actually, the 505TH, part of the 82nd Airbourne Division, has done better fighting than any outfit in the theatre. They make the regular infantry look sick!

Today we had a parade, and the men were awarded citations for combat achievements. Some of the men here are really covered with various ribbons and medals.

As yet I have not been given a definite position in the company so I don't know just what I will be. For the time being I guess I will do anything and everything.

Just to make sure you have my correct address I shall print it plainly below. I will keep this one for some time I'm sure!

Pvt. Earl G. Thurman – 34760054
Co. "G" 505th Prcht. Inf. A.P.O. 469
c/o P.M. New York, N.Y.

I trust that you and Daddy are feeling fine.

Lots of love,
Gene

Mrs. E. V. Thurman
304 N. Cheney St
East Point, Georgia

Pvt Earl G. Thurman 34760054
Co "G" 505 Prcht Inf A.P.O. 469
c/o PM New York N.Y.

July 30th, 1944

Dear Mother

As normal I have little of interest to write. Everything has been going along in a normal manner. I have been doing quite a bit of bike riding in the evenings, riding as much as twenty five miles at a time. I enjoy it very much, as the country-side here is really beautiful. I am most fortunate to be here. The other day, or rather evening, I met a British "Tommie" in town and we had a pleasant time together. I may see him again if the situation permits. I like the English very much. The boys seem to be much more polite and courteous than the Americans.

I hope you are receiving my mail promptly by now and I guess I will be hearing from you soon.

Love,

Gene

"I met a British Tommie"

The term "Tommy" originates from the slang word for a British solider named "Tommy Atkins", which is believed to have derived from a pamphlet from the war office in 1815, naming Private Tommy Atkins as an example of how a soldier should be turned out. The Duke of Wellington may have suggested the name, in memory of a soldier from his regiment who had been killed in action in 1794 in Flanders. The term was more prolific during the First World War, where German soldiers would call out "Tommy" in no man's land if they wanted to make conversation with a British solider.

Mrs E. V. Thurman   Pvt. Earl G. Thurman
304 N. Cheney St   A.S.N. 34760054
East Point, Ga   Co "G" 505th Prcht Inf. A.P.O. 465
c/o P.M. New York. N.Y.

August 3rd, 1944

Dear Mother,

I'm sorry I am a bit late in writing, but we have been rather busy lately and I haven't had too much time off. When I get a pass in the evening I like to go out on my bike and ride through the country. This is really as lovely a place as I ever saw, just to be more farming country. I guess the damp climate makes things grow better, for you never see a bare spot of land anywhere.

We are having a bit of training now, but nothing tough just yet. It is just enough to keep me busy.

The food is still good, and I'm feeling fine. In general, I actually like it over here. Hope you and Daddy are feeling fine.

Lots of love,

Gene

Mrs E.V. Thurman
304 N. Cheney St
East Point, Georgia

Pvt. Earl G. Thurman
Co "G" Prcht. Inf. A.P.O. 496
c/o P.M. New York N.Y.

August 7th, 1944

Dear Mother

I received my first V-mail from you today, and I was glad to get the news from home. It's fine to know that Nell is getting along well in New York. She seems to be leading a charmed life there.

Things are still going fine here with me. We are not being worked too hard, and are still well fed. Yesterday, Sunday, we had chicken, and all that goes with it including ice cream. I really enjoyed that meal.

Yesterday afternoon I went for a bike ride, and rode about forty miles. It was a lot of fun, and good exercise, too.

The weather here is very nice now. It is normally cloudy until noon, then the sun comes out and warms things up a bit.

Hope you and Daddy are fine,

Love,
Gene

Mrs E.V. Thurman
304 N. Cheney St.
East Point, Georgia

ASN 34760054
Pvt. Earl G. Thurman
Co "G" 505th Prcht Inf.
A.P.O. 469
c/o P.M. New York, N.Y.

August 10th, 1944

Dear Mother,

I hope things are going well with you at home. I haven't heard from you since I got that one V-mail letter, but I don't guess it is any fault of yours. The mail just isn't prompt at all when you change address as often as I do. Probably by the time you get his I will also be getting yours regularly.

Today we had a division parade, and were received by none other than General Eisenhower himself, He seemed well pleased at our appearance, and gave a little "pup talk" congratulating the 82nd on its action in France. Incidentally our battalion was judged the best in the division on its appearance. We had a similar parade Saturday, and we were also judged the best then. Not Bad! I have not done so much in the way of amusement lately, other than bike riding and one "cinema" I get a lot of pleasure from riding around in the country, as I have mentioned before, and often ride twenty or more miles in an evening. I went to a nearby town and saw Basil Rathbone in a "Sherlock Holmes" picture last night. Oddly enough, practically all of the pictures here are American.

"Gone With the Wind" is to be here sometime soon.

The food is fine now and with the doughnuts & coffee we can buy in the evenings we make out fine. I'll be getting fat if I'm not careful!

Lots of love to you & Daddy,

Gene

American General, Dwight D. Eisenhower, supreme commander of the allied forces in Europe, visited Hungerford common West Berkshire, England on August 10th, 1944, overseeing a parade of an estimated 18,000 personnel, including members of the 82nd Airborne.

Mrs E.V. Thurman
304 N. Cheney St.
East Point, Georgia

Pvt. Earl G. Thurman
ASN 34760054
Co "G" 505th Prcht Inf. A.P.O. 469
c/o P.M. New York, N.Y.

August 14th, 1944

Dear Mother,

I hope you will forgive the slight delay in writing, but I have been detached from my company for additional training and am at a different camp now. This is only temporary, and my address is the same. They will send my mail here from my outfit.

The weather is very pleasant, and we have had quite a bit of sunshine lately.

I still have my bike and it is quite a convenience here. We have a long walk to the mess hall, and we are also a long way from town. If I ever get a pass it will come in handy.

From what I have seen of the camp so far I think I am going to like it here. Hope things are fine at home.

Lots of love,

Gene

34760054

Mrs E.V. Thurman
304 N. Cheney St.
East Point, Georgia

Pvt. Earl G. Thurman
Co "G" 505 Prcht. Inf. A.P.O. 469
c/o P.M. New York, N.Y.

August 16th, 1944

Dear Mother.

I was indeed glad to receive your letter of August 6th today. It is the most recent news I've received since I've been over here. That is, from home. We are pretty well up on the news as far as the war goes, seems to be going good, don't you think?

The weather is very pleasant, and things in general are very nice here.

I'm glad Nell liked New York so well and had such good luck there. She is with you now I guess and having a well deserved vacation unless you are keeping her busy!

I still have my bike, but I don't have so much time to use it now. I think maybe I will next week.

Give my love to all.

Devotedly,

Gene

Mrs E.V. Thurman
304 N. Cheney St.
East Point, Georgia

Pvt. Earl G. Thurman
Co "G" 505 Prcht Inf A.P.O. 469
c/o P.M. New York, NY

August 21st, 1944

Dear Mother,

I hope things are well with you. It seems like a long time since I've heard from you but I know there is nothing to do about that.

The weather here is not best just now, as we have had several rainy days lately. I think this English mud is even worse than Georgia red clay if that be possible.

I haven't been doing much biking lately due to the weather conditions and lack of ambition. The country here is pretty, although it is all much the same, small pastures and fields divided by hedgerows.

This is really all I have to write this evening, I guess.
Give my love to daddy.

Devotedly,
Gene

Mrs E.V. Thurman
304 N. Cheney St.
East Point, Georgia

Pvt Earl G. Thurman
Co. "G" 505th Prcht Inf. A.P.O. 469
c/o P.M. New York, N.Y.

August 25th, 1944

Dear Mother

Here I am writing again with nothing to say just trying to keep morale up on the home front. Last night I got a letter from you, Nell and Lenie. I am answering yours first, and hope to have time and ambition to answer the other two. I find it very difficult to write these days, with so little to say. I do have plenty of time just now. I hope I haven't been too bad about writing. I hear from Jenelle a lot, and she asks me to always write you before I write her. I guess she knows how a mother feels, as Mrs Witaker has lost a son in action so recently.

The weather here is still "all wet," but I'm doing fine where I am. The bad weather gives us a lot more spare time.

I'll write again soon.

Love,

Gene

ASN 34760054

Mrs E.V.Thurman
304 N.Cheney Street
East Point, Georgia

Pvt. Earl G.Thurman
Co "G" Prcht. Inf. A.P.O. 469
c/o P.M. New YORK, N.Y.

August 25th, 1944

Dear Daddy,

Yes, I have finally gotten around writing you I would have before but since there is so little to write I just consider writing to mother as enough for you both. Actually, one letter a month would be sufficient to tell you all the news I have.

I'm glad you were able to attend at least one day of the singing, and I certainly would like to have been there. Maybe next year there will be a good old three day singing again. I hope I can be there, too. I don't think the war will last that much longer, but we can't be sure of being home that soon. Somebody will have to stay over here.

This is about all I have to say I guess. Hope everything is well with you.

Lots of love,
Gene

"Three day singing"

Refers to singing Hymns over the period of Maundy Thursday, Good Friday, and Holy Saturday. The three days are all part of one great and mystical service.

Mr E.V. Thurman
304 N. Cheney St
East Point, Georgia

Pvt Earl G. Thurman
A.S.N. 34760054
Co"G"505 Prcht. Inf. A.P.O.469
c/o P.M. New York N.Y.

September 8th, 1944

Dear Daddy,

Just thought I would let you know I'm still "thinking of you, " by dropping you a short note. Things are going along pretty nice these days, as far as I'm concerned. We are having life easy enough, and this morning the sun is out. We have had a lot of cool and rainy weather in the past couple of weeks.

England is still a very pretty place, but the new has worn off now, and I don't go out much. I go to town once in a while to the show, and that is about all lately. I don't have the bike anymore, so naturally I don't do much riding.

I hope things are going nice at home these days. Go to a singing for me sometime soon.

Lots of love,

Gene

Mrs E.V. Thurman
304 N. Cheney St.
East Point, Georgia

Pvt Earl G. Thurman
Co. "G" 505th Prcht Inf. A.P.O. 469
c/o P.M. New York, N.Y.

Sep. 9th, 1944

Dear Mother,

I hope you will forgive me for not writing, but it is something out of my hands this time, for I simply haven't had a chance. I guess by now you are about used to going without mail, but it's a good thing, for it will probably be that way for the duration.

Things are going pretty nice here, and I don't guess I have anything to comp-lain about. It has been cool and raining lately but not really objectionable. We have a nice camp here, even though we do live in tents, some of the camps are terribly muddy in this kind of weather.

I'm glad things are going so well in the old home town. I hope Nell is situated in Chicago by now, I'm glad she was able to spent a month at home with you.

Love to you & Daddy,

Gene

Earl has written the date as the 13th of September, but the postal stamp is the 12th of September.

SEP 12, 1944
Pvt Earl G. Thurman
A.S.N/ 34760054
Co "G" 505 Prcht Inf.
APO 469 c/o PM.
New York, N.Y.
Mrs. E.V. Thurman
304 N. Cheney St
East Point, Georgia

PASSED BY ARMY EXAMINER

Wednesday A.M.
September 13, 1944

Dear Mother

I have little to say as I have already written you a V-mail this morning. I wouldn't have done so but at the time I forgot about the money orders.

As you can see, I don't spend much on this side of the ocean, and have saved quite a bit out of my last three months pay. Enclosed you will find two one hundred dollar money orders, to be deposited with my account, or rather with yours as I don't think I have one. I shall send home as much as I can each month and maybe by the time I get home I will have enough to do something with. I don't know exactly how much I have now, but I'll let you keep up with it. If Nell needs any don't hesitate to let her have it. I will write and tell her to ask you anytime she does.

Love to you and Daddy,
From,
Gene

V-mail dated 13th, September 1944. A letter home before action as the 82nd Airbourne dropped into Holland on the 17th of September 1944.

	34760059
Miss Nell Thurman	Pvt. Earl G. Thurman
64 E. Van Boren St.	Co "G" 505 Prcht. Inf. A.P.O. 469
Chicago 5, Illinois	c/o P.M. New York, N.Y.

Dear Nell,

Yes, I have at last come to life long enough to drop you a line. It's not really that way however, I simply haven't had a chance to write for several days. I have my hands full tonight trying to catch up on correspondence.

I'm glad you were able to be with mother for a few weeks. I guess that visit helped more than any amount of medicine would. I hope she is doing as well as I'm led to believe.

How does it feel to be back in the "windy," and noisy, city again? Are you living at the same place, or have you given them the air?

I'm getting along fine now, busy but not working hard enough to hurt myself. You probably guessed as much.

I'll write again soon Love,

Gene

HOLLAND

OPERATION MARKET GARDEN

Mrs E.V. Thurman	Pvt. Earl G. Thurman
304 N. Cheney St.	A.S.N. 34780054
East Point, Ga	Co "G" 505th Prcht Inf A.P.O. 469
	c/o P.M. New York N.Y.

September 30th, 1944

Dear Mother,

I know it's been quite some time since you last heard from me, but I don't guess I need any excuse this time. I only hope this little note cheers you up a bit.

I'm in Holland now as you may have guessed, but things are not too bad. I have fared quite well so far, and I don't think you need to worry to much about my safety.

I hope things are going well at home. I have received several of your letters here and certainly enjoyed them.

Lots of love,

Gene

Mrs E.V. Thurman
304 N. Cheney St.
East Point, Ga

Pvt. Earl G. Thurman
A.S.N. 34780054
Co "G" 505th Prcht Inf A.P.O. 469
c/o P.M. New York N.Y.

Holland – Oct 9th, 1944

Dear mother,
This is just another short note to let you know that I'm still alright, and in the same little country of windmills and wooden shoes. I've seen some of both since I got here too. This is really a beautiful and interesting country although the war hasn't helped things and there are a lot of fruit trees about, apples, pear, and peach. The food ration is well in hand.
I enjoyed the letter from you with the clippings and I was also very much interested in your "Florida" trip. You are welcome to my money, and please take whatever you need of it – that two hundred dollars got to you, didn't it?
You may be in Newman by the time this gets to you. Give my love to all the folks,

As always,
Gene

Mr E.V. Thurman
304 N. Cheney St.
East Point, Ga

Pvt. Earl G. Thurman
A.S.N. 34780054
Co "G" 505th Prcht Inf A.P.O. 469
c/o P.M. New York N.Y.

Holland – Oct 9th, 1944

Dear Daddy,

Well I guess you think I've lost my pen by now but I haven't you see. It's just that conditions are not for writing these days. I will try to write a little more often in the future.

I guess mother is in Newman by now and I hope she is enjoying her visit there. If her letter come's with this don't hesitate to read it too, for it is meant for you also.

Things are going O.K. now, considering the war. There is nothing wrong with me now that a good shave, shower, and sirloin wouldn't cure: A day of good singing might help, too:

I hope you are getting along fine these days, and I hope your recent birthday was a happy one.

Lots of love,

Gene

A let up in censorship lets Earl tell his family he's in Holland:

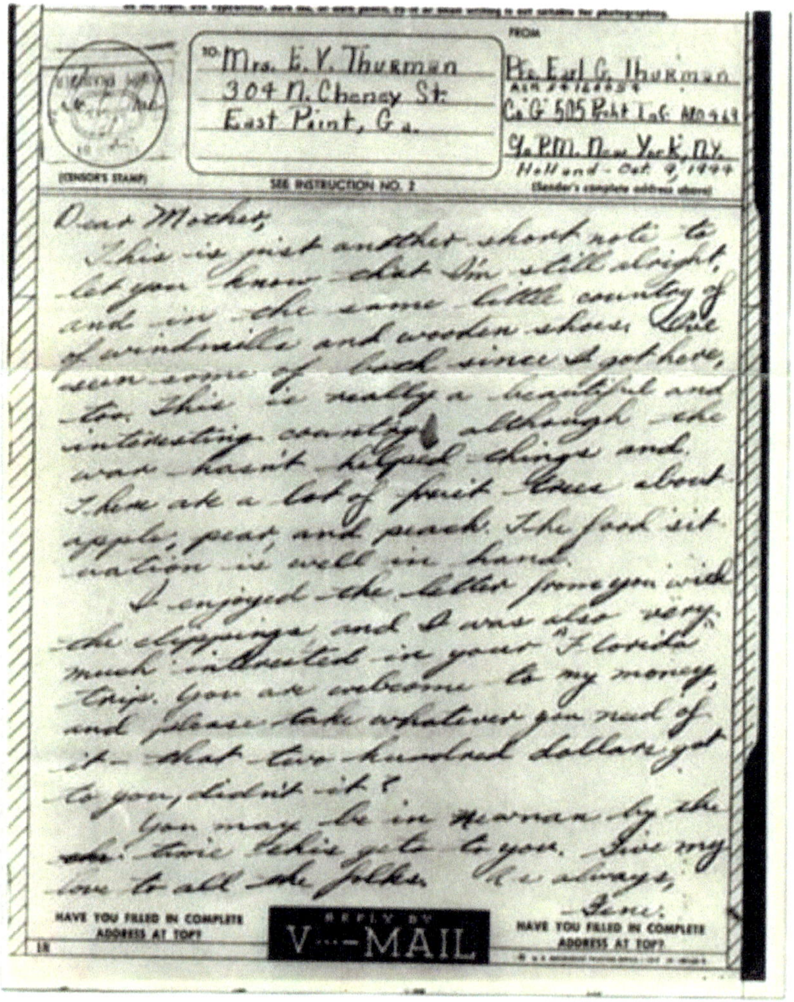

CENSOR'S STAMP

TO: Mrs. E. V. Thurman
304 N. Cheney St.
East Point, Ga.

SEE INSTRUCTION NO. 2

FROM: Pfc. Earl G. Thurman
Co. "G" 505 Prcht Inf. APO 469
% P.M. New York, N.Y.
Holland - Oct. 9, 1944
(Sender's complete address above)

Dear Mother,

This is just another short note to let you know that I'm still alright, and in the same little country of of windmills and wooden shoes. I've seen some of both since I got here, too. This is really a beautiful and interesting country, although the war hasn't helped things and. There are a lot of fruit trees about apple, pear, and peach. The food situation is well in hand.

I enjoyed the letter from you with the clippings and I was also very much interested in your "Florida" trip. You are welcome to my money, and please take whatever you need of it — that two hundred dollars got to you, didn't it?

You may be in Newnan by the ~~the~~ time this gets to you. Give my love to all the folks. As always,

Gene.

HAVE YOU FILLED IN COMPLETE ADDRESS AT TOP?

REPLY BY V---MAIL

HAVE YOU FILLED IN COMPLETE ADDRESS AT TOP?

Miss Nell Thurman
Allerton Hotel
Chicago 11, Illinois

34760054
Pfc. Earl G. Thurman
Co "G" 505 Prcht. Inf. A.P.O. 469
c/o P.M. New York, N.Y.

Holland – October 13th, 1944

Dear Nell

I hope you will for give your baby brother for not writing sooner, but I wasn't sure of your address until recently, and I haven't been doing a lot of writing anyway.

There is little I can tell you about life in Holland, but things are going very well. Tell you all about it some of these days.

From yours & Mothers letters, you seem to be doing quite well this year, although I'm sure you are busy as a bee. I hope you don't run yourself down without realising it. I sent Mother some money recently and if you need any you are welcome to it. Don't hesitate.

If Helen is at school this year, tell her Hello for me and that Holland is a pretty country full of swell people!

Be Sweet.

Love,

Gene

ENGLAND

Earl was wounded in Action on the 17th of October 1944, this letter was written before a Telegram was sent informing his family of his situation. But due to the time it took to send and deliver mail the Telegram most likely would have arrived first, note the change in handwriting.

Mrs E.V. Thurman	Pvt. Earl G. Thurman
304 N. Cheney St.	Co "G" 505th Prcht Inf. A.P.O. 469
East Point, Ga	c/o P.M. New York N.Y.

October 25th, 1944

Dear Mother

I'm sorry I can't write a more legible letter, but as you can guess I'm using the wrong Hand. By now you may have been notified that I've been wounded, but I just wanted to write and let you know I'm being well taken care of and am doing fine. Just don't worry one bit about me, please. There is no reason.
I hope things are going well at home.

Love to all,
Gene

P.S. Looks like a first – grader!

P.S. Looks like a first – grader!

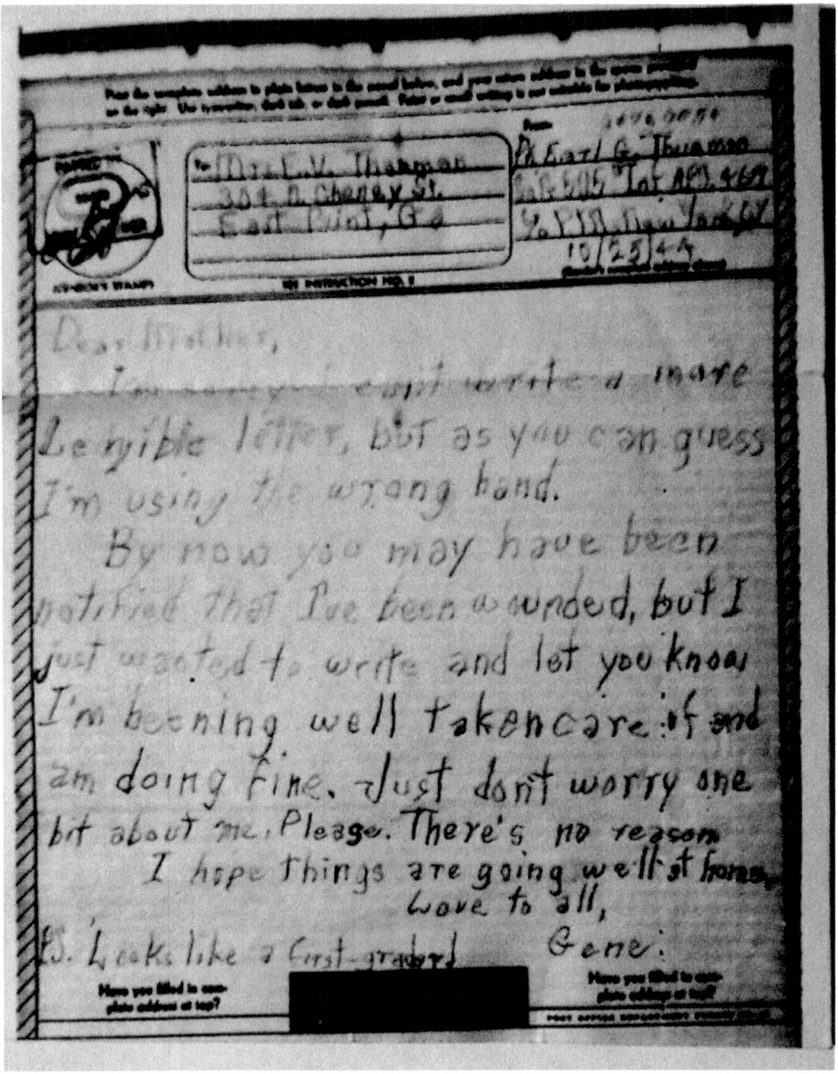

To Mrs. E.V. Thompson
354 N. Cheney St.
East Point, Ga.

From Pfc Earl G. Thompson
505th Inf APO 469
c/o PM New York NY
10/25/44

Dear Mother,

I'm sorry I can't write a more legible letter, but as you can guess I'm using the wrong hand.

By now you may have been notified that I've been wounded, but I just wanted to write and let you know I'm beening well takencare of and am doing fine. Just don't worry one bit about me. Please. There's no reason

I hope things are going well at home.

Love to all,

Gene:

P.S. Looks like a first-grader!

Have you filled in complete address at top?

[redacted]

Have you filled in complete address at top?

November 5th, 1944, Telegram notification, Wounded in Action:

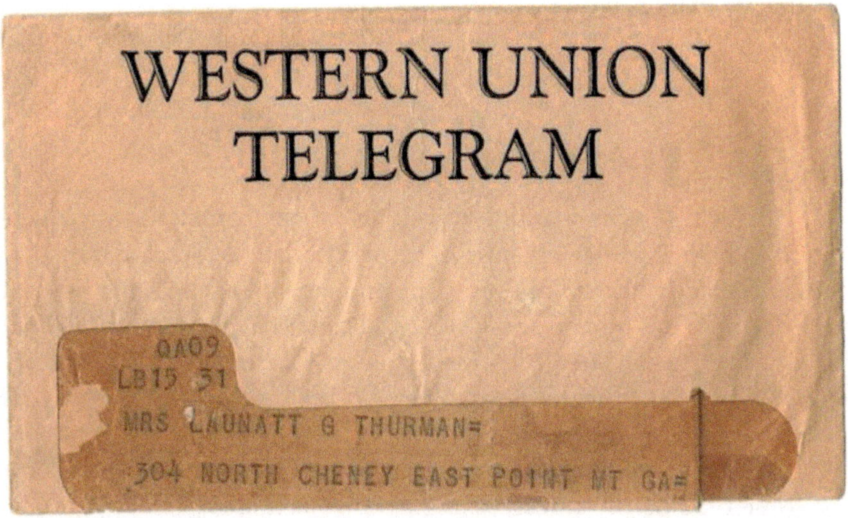

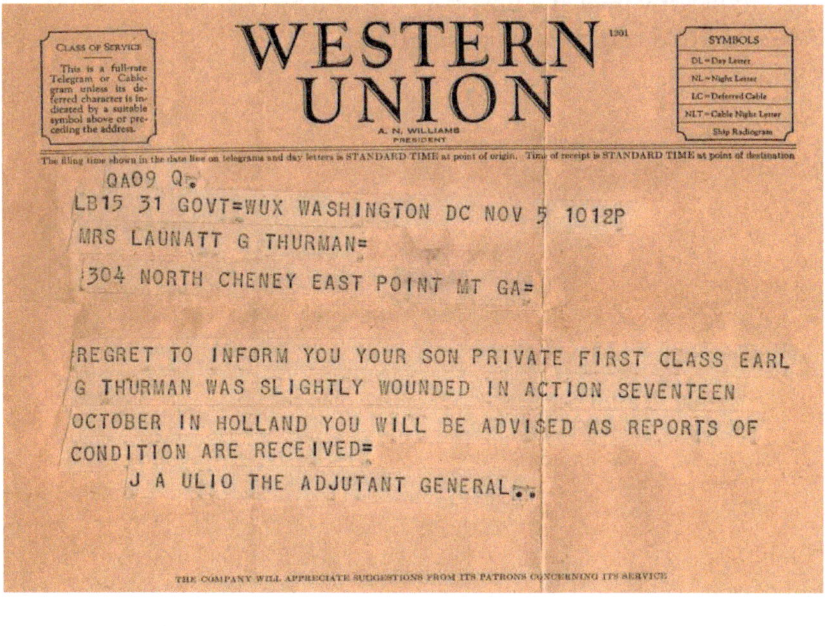

CLASS OF SERVICE
This is a full-rate Telegram or Cablegram unless its deferred character is indicated by a suitable symbol above or preceding the address.

WESTERN UNION
1201
A. N. WILLIAMS
PRESIDENT

SYMBOLS
DL=Day Letter
NL=Night Letter
LC=Deferred Cable
NLT=Cable Night Letter
Ship Radiogram

The filing time shown in the date line on telegrams and day letters is STANDARD TIME at point of origin. Time of receipt is STANDARD TIME at point of destination

QA09 Q.
LB15 31 GOVT=WUX WASHINGTON DC NOV 5 1012P
MRS LAUNATT G THURMAN=
304 NORTH CHENEY EAST POINT MT GA=

REGRET TO INFORM YOU YOUR SON PRIVATE FIRST CLASS EARL G THURMAN WAS SLIGHTLY WOUNDED IN ACTION SEVENTEEN OCTOBER IN HOLLAND YOU WILL BE ADVISED AS REPORTS OF CONDITION ARE RECEIVED=
J A ULIO THE ADJUTANT GENERAL.

THE COMPANY WILL APPRECIATE SUGGESTIONS FROM ITS PATRONS CONCERNING ITS SERVICE

Mrs E.V. Thurman
304 N. Cheney St.
East Point, Ga

34760054
Pvt. Earl G. Thurman
Det of Patient's
4190 U.S. Army Hospital Plant, APO 209
c/o P.M. N.Y., N.Y.

Nov. 12th, 1944

Dear Mother,

Well, I guess you tire of waiting for my somewhat infrequent letters. There is really very little in them, after all, just something to let you and Daddy know I'm doing fine and am still at the same hospital in England. I am up and about now and can go to the movies, Chapel, or anywhere else. They even make me go to the "mess hall" for my chow! Not being able to use my "left" is inconvenient, but I have no real trouble.

I have no idea of what is going on at home, and I guess it will be some time before I hear a thing from you. It always takes, a month or so to get any mail at a hospital.

I hope you and Daddy are fine.

Love,

Gene

Another example of his handwriting after injury:

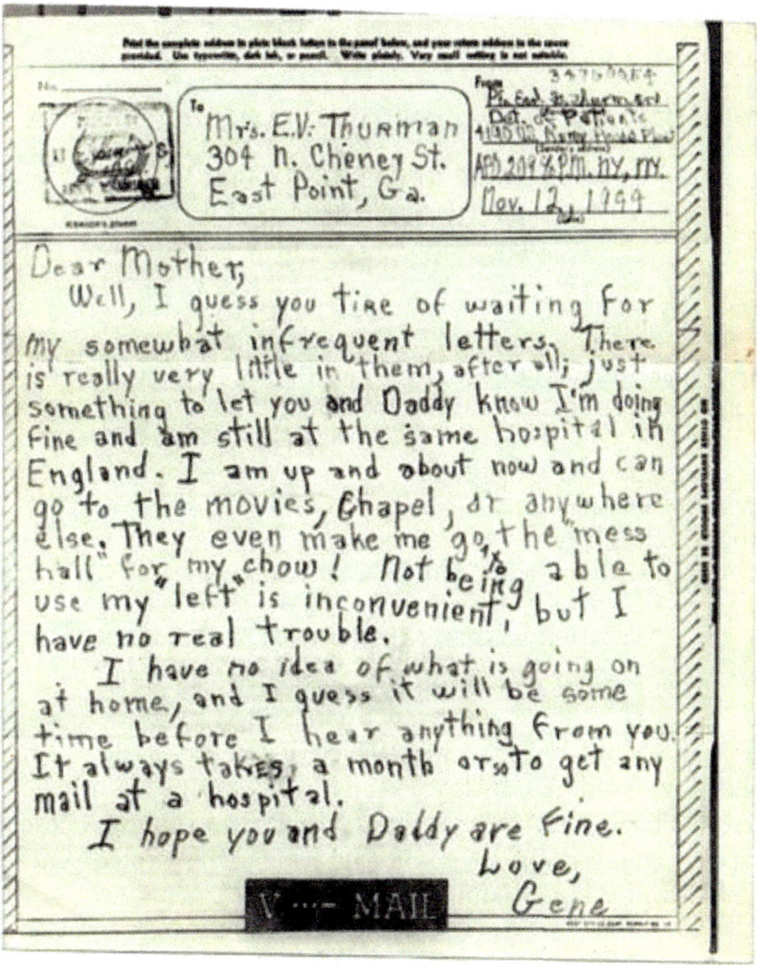
To
Mrs. E.V. Thurman
304 N. Cheney St.
East Point, Ga.

APO 209 % P.M. NY, NY.
Nov. 12, 1944

Dear Mother;

Well, I guess you tire of waiting for my somewhat infrequent letters. There is really very little in them, after all; just something to let you and Daddy know I'm doing fine and am still at the same hospital in England. I am up and about now and can go to the movies, Chapel, or anywhere else. They even make me go to the "mess hall" for my chow! Not being able to use my "left" is inconvenient, but I have no real trouble.

I have no idea of what is going on at home, and I guess it will be some time before I hear anything from you. It always takes a month or so to get any mail at a hospital.

I hope you and Daddy are fine.

Love,
Gene

V---MAIL

Transcription of a report made by Earl on how he was wounded in action, the information was released to a local journalist in Earl's hometown of East Point, Georgia who worked for The Atlanta Constitution Newspaper.

CONFIDENTIAL

PUBLIC RELATIONS OFFICE
83RD (U.S.) General Hospital
ETO USA APO 209
17 November 1944

Release No. 82

TO: Public Relations Office Hq., U.K. Base Section, CZ, APO 413
Attention: Capt. BERGER

Date of casualty: 17 October 1944
Date entered hospital: 4 November 1944
Written home: Yes
Received letter from home: No

WOUNDED EAST POINT SOLDIER RECOVERING IN ENGLAND

THE 83RD GENERAL HOSPITAL, ENGLAND

The story of the surprise with which Paratroop soldiers landed in Holland was told here by Private First-Class Earl G. Thurman, 20, of 304 N. Chaney St., East Point, Georgia, who is convalescing of shrapnel wounds of the chest and right hand in this United States Army general hospital in England.

Pfc. Thurman who has been awarded the purple heart for wounds received in action, "is recovering from his wounds very satisfactorily and is up and around the ward taking part in different activities, "said ward surgeon Captain Brune J. Peters of Wauwatosa, Wisconsin. "When our company dropped into Holland early on a Sunday afternoon we captured German soldiers riding bicycles with the Dutch girls on the handlebars," Pfc. Thurman told. "The ariel invasion went off perfectly and my company captured our objective of a small town with little opposition. For a month we moved slowly cleaning out one small town and going into a defensive position before moving on to the west. German artillery fire was harassing us most of the time.

"Another soldier and myself were carrying some radio equipment forward to the front lines while in a holding position when enemy fire forced us into a ditch for cover," the East Point paratrooper continued. "A 88 mm shell struck in a tree above throwing shrapnel in all directions and we were both hit. The company aid man was with us right away, administered first aid and had us on our way back to a field hospital. I was brought to England by air."

Formerly employed by the Westinghouse Electric Co., Atlanta Plant, Pfc Thurman is the son of Mr. and Mrs. E.V. Thurman who reside at the East Point address.

END

Lt. John H. Mills, MAC, PRO
T/3 R.E. Gruner

Unit Correspondent

Released To:

Atlanta, Georgia. Constitution
Journal

East Point, Georgia. Atlanta Suburban Reporter

Confidential report from Earl regarding his injuries:

CONFIDENTIAL

PUBLIC RELATIONS OFFICE
83rd (U.S.) General Hospital
ETO USA APO 209

17 November 1944

Release No. 82

TO: Public Relations Office Hq., U. K. Base Section, CZ, APO 413
Attention: Capt. BERGER

Date of casualty: 17 October 1944
Date entered hospital: 4 November 1944
Written home: Yes
Received letter from home: No

WOUNDED EAST POINT SOLDIER RECOVERING IN ENGLAND

THE 83RD GENERAL HOSPITAL, ENGLAND—The story of the surprise with which paratroop soldiers landed in Holland was told here by Private First Class Earl G. Thurman, 20, of 304 N. Chaney St., East Point, Georgia, who is convalescing of shrapnel wounds of the chest and right hand in this United States Army general hospital in England.

Pfc. Thurman, who has been awarded the Purple Heart for wounds received in action, "is recovering from his wounds very satisfactorily and is up and around the ward taking part in different activities," said ward surgeon Captain Bruno J. Peters of Wauwatosa, Wisconsin.

"When our company dropped into Holland early on a Sunday afternoon we captured German soldiers riding bicycles with the Dutch girls on the handlebars," Pfc. Thurman told. "The aerial invasion went off perfectly and my company captured our objective of a small town with little opposition. For a month we moved slowly cleaning out one small town and going into a defensive position before moving on to the next. German artillery fire was harassing us most of the time.

"Another soldier and myself were carrying some radio equipment forward to the front lines while in a holding position when enemy fire forced us into a ditch for cover," the East Point paratrooper continued. "A 88 mm shell struck in a tree above us throwing shrapnel in all directions and we were both hit. The company aid man was with us right away, adminstered first aid and had us on our way back to a field hospital. I was brought to England by air."

Formerly employed by the Westinghouse Electric Co., Atlanta Plant, Pfc. Thurman is the son of Mr. and Mrs. S. V. Thurman who reside at the East Point address.

END.

Lt. John H. Mills, MAC, PRO

T/3 R. E. Gruner
Unit Correspondent

Release To:

Atlanta, Georgia. Constitution
Journal

East Point, Georgia . Atlanta Surburban Reporter

In Earl's letter dated December 16th, 1944, although his wounds were quite serious, if not life threatening initially, you can sense by his writing that he tries to explain his injuries are not very serious, playing them down stop his family from worrying, especially his mother.

"I guess you are convinced that I'm feeling fine now. My hand is doing O.K., and my chest feels almost as good as ever. They removed the shrapnel about three weeks ago, and did a swell job of it. I was out of bed almost as soon as I returned from the oper. Room, and on pass a week later! I just hope you feel half as good as I!"

Earl did receive shrapnel wounds believed to come from a German artillery 88mm shell, wounding him seriously enough to warrant an operation, to remove shrapnel from his thorax, chest, possible amputation of his index finger, the medical card reads "Amp, traumatic, complete" and a moderate laceration to his third finger.

Emergency medical tag, detailing Earls injuries:

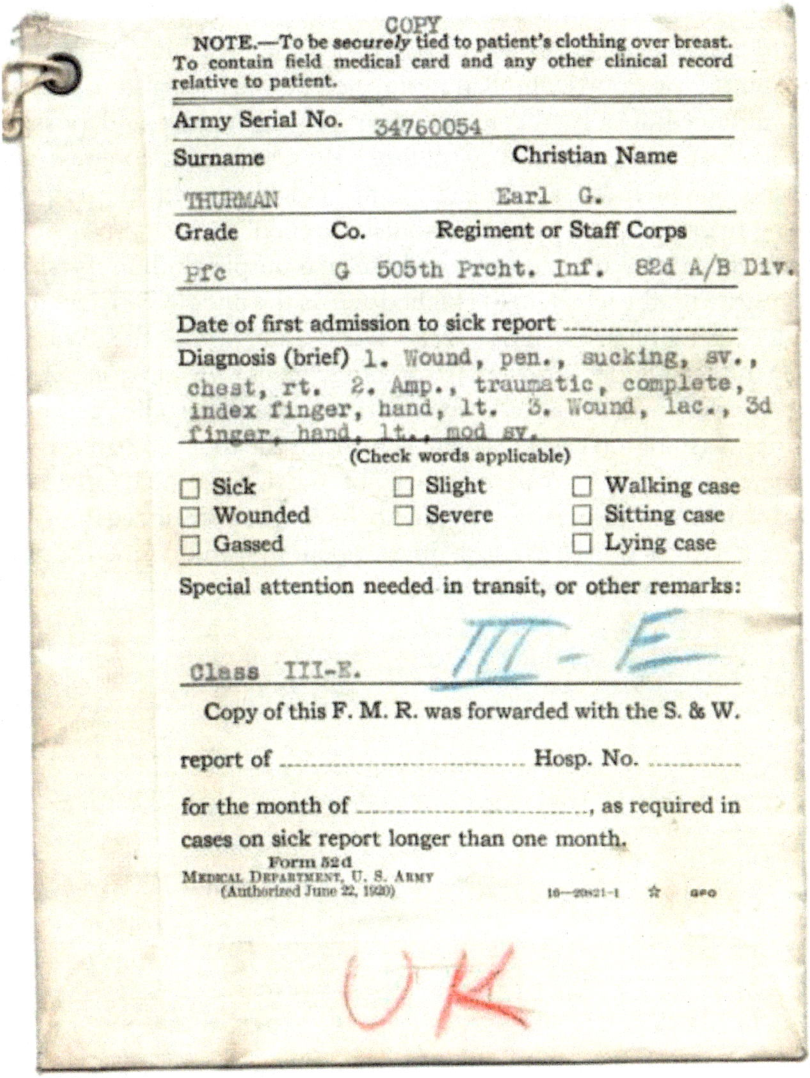

COPY

NOTE.—To be *securely* tied to patient's clothing over breast. To contain field medical card and any other clinical record relative to patient.

Army Serial No. 34760054

Surname THURMAN Christian Name Earl G.

Grade Pfc Co. G Regiment or Staff Corps 505th Prcht. Inf. 82d A/B Div.

Date of first admission to sick report ....

Diagnosis (brief) 1. Wound, pen., sucking, sv., chest, rt. 2. Amp., traumatic, complete, index finger, hand, lt. 3. Wound, lac., 3d finger, hand, lt., mod sv.

(Check words applicable)

☐ Sick ☐ Slight ☐ Walking case
☐ Wounded ☐ Severe ☐ Sitting case
☐ Gassed ☐ Lying case

Special attention needed in transit, or other remarks:

Class III-E. III-E

Copy of this F. M. R. was forwarded with the S. & W.

report of .... Hosp. No. ....

for the month of ...., as required in cases on sick report longer than one month.

Form 52d
Medical Department, U. S. Army
(Authorized June 22, 1920)

16—20821-1 ☆ GPO

OK

The Purple Heart mentioned in the letter to Captain Bercher from the public relations Office on November 17th, 1944, started life as the "Badge of Military Merit". It is America's oldest military award for courage and was introduced towards the end of the American War of Independence in 1782. General George Washington wanted recognition for troops who had performed heroic acts, also to be seen as a morale boost in the hope of preventing unrest and possible rebellion of the troops. At the time, the American congress was running out of funds after many years of fighting with the English, leaving troops unpaid, hungry, and disheartened.

The original award was made from a purple cloth in the shape of a heart with the word merit stitched across the middle. Washington's "Badge of Military Merit" was faded out after the War of Independence ended. On February 22nd, 1932, Washington's 200th birthday the medal was re-introduced, featuring a profile picture of George Washington's head. Today it is one of the most recognized and respected awards given to members of the U.S. armed forces, for military merit, awarded to those who have been wounded or killed during enemy action. It is a solemn distinction, meaning the recipient has sacrificed themselves in the line of duty.

1943 American Emblem Company Purple Heart medal, made from bronze with gold gilt.

Throughout the Second World War, the American Red Cross volunteers provided aid and comfort to all members of the military service which included providing passionate support for injured troops. Amongst Earl's collection is a Red Cross draw string convalescent kit bag produced by the Pittsburgh, Penna Chapter which he may have received in an English Hospital to boost his morale.

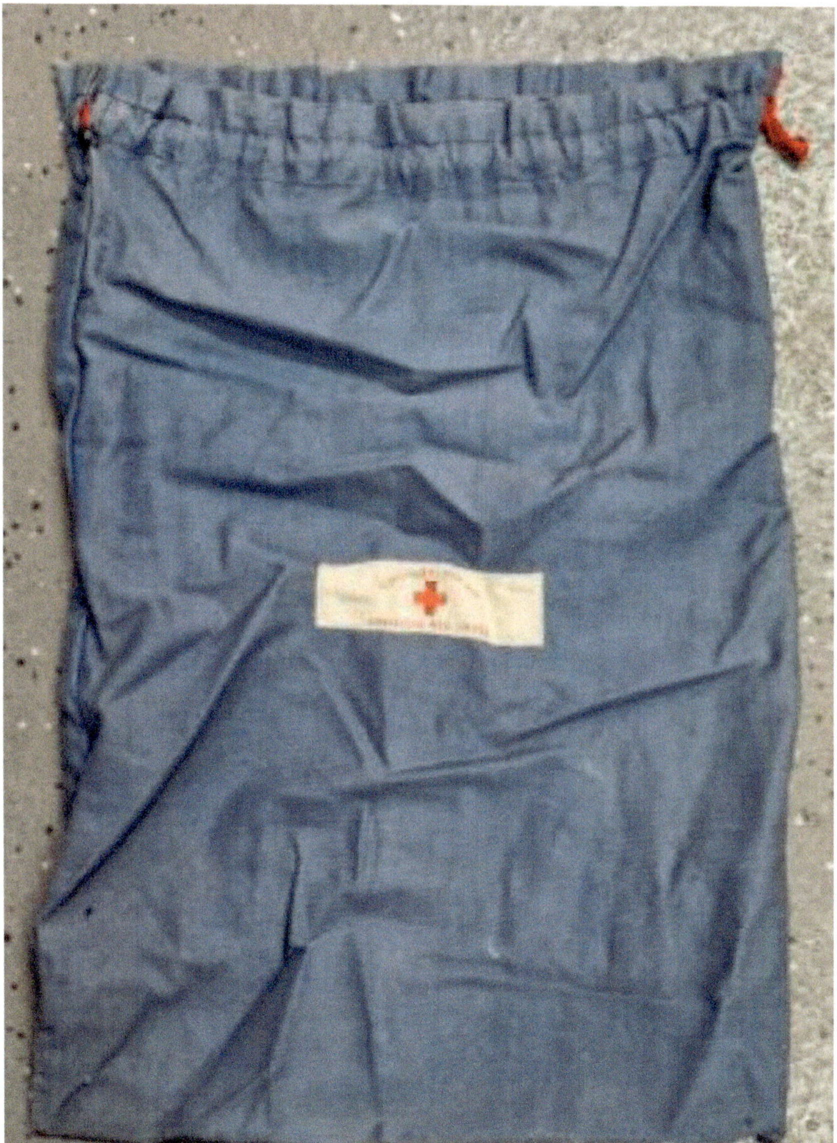

Mrs E.V. Thurman
304 N. Cheney St.
East Point, Ga

Pfc. Earl G. Thurman ASN 34760054
ASN 34760054
Det. Of Patients
4189 U.S. Army Hospital Plant
A.P.O. 209 c/o P.M. N.Y. N.Y.

Sun P.M. 26 Nov

Dear Mother,

Well here is another mess of a letter for you. My hand writing is much better now, and I can do a bit of writing. I hope it isn't too hard to read.

I am at another hospital now but the address is almost the same. I hope my mail catches me soon. I have received a package from Jenelle and one from the Bishops but no letters.

At the other hospital a sergeant took down an account of my little accident, which was to be sent to the Atlanta paper and the reporter.

I hope everything is fine at home now. I'll write Daddy in a few days, when hand is steadier.

Love to all,

Gene

Mr E.V.Thurman
304 N. Cheney St.
East Point, Ga

Pfc. Earl G. Thurman
A.S.N. 34760054
Det. Of Patients
4189 U.S. Army Hospital Plant
A.P.O. 209 c/o P.M. N.Y. N.Y.

Nov 29, 1944

Dear Daddy,

I'm still at the same hospital, and doing fine. As yet I have received no mail, but I've gotten several packages, including a delicious fruit cake from Judy. I will indeed be glad to hear from you and mother.

The weather here isn't so bad, although it is rainy. I'm indoors most of the time anyway, but I hope to get out some soon. I was out several afternoons at the other hospital, and it was fun to walk through the pretty English countryside after being in for so long.

I guess this is all for now. Hope you're feeling fine.

Love,
Gene

Mrs E. V. Thurman
304 N. Cheney St.
East Point, Ga

Pfc. Earl G. Thurman
A.S.N. 34760054
Det. Of Patients
4189 U.S. Army Hospital Plant
A.P.O. 209 c/o P.M. N.Y. N.Y.

December 6, 1944

Dear Mother,

The long awaited letter from you finally arrived yesterday. I was relieved to know everything was alright, and that you had heard from me. I also received a letter from Babby in my outfit, so I guess my old mail will catch me soon. I hope so.

Things are going fine now. I feel just as good as ever. We are continually "cursing" the English weather, as it rains so often, but it really isn't so bad for this time of year.

I guess you and Daddy will be rather lonely this Christmas as it is the first one Nell & I have both been absent from. Maybe the next will be better!

Lots of love,

Gene

Mrs E. V. Thurman
304 N. Cheney St.
East Point, Ga

Pfc. Earl G. Thurman
A.S.N. 34760054
Det. Of Patients
4189 U.S. Army Hospital Plant
A.P.O. 209 c/o P.M. N.Y. N.Y.

December 8, 1944

Dear Mother,

Just another short note telling you that I'm still around and doing fine. I was very happy to receive another letter from you the other day. I'm glad to hear that you are feeling so good, but please don't make that mistake as you often have, of out doing yourself. I hope you know better by now! I was in town again last night and I went to the Methodist Church, a very pretty building and a very nice service to which I was invited. They had a guest singer who was very good and in keeping with English customs "Tea"

I guess by now you are at home once more. Here's hoping that things are going well, and may continue to do so.

Give my love to Daddy.

As ever,
Gene

Mrs E. V. Thurman
304 N. Cheney St.
East Point, Ga

Pfc. Earl G. Thurman
A.S.N. 34760054
Det. Of Patients
4189 U.S. Army Hospital Plant
A.P.O. 209 c/o P.M. N.Y. N.Y.

December 8, 1944

Dear Mother,

This is just another little note to let you know that I'm still at the same hospital and doing fine. I haven't heard from you since the letter I received at the first of the week. I guess the mail is just naturally slow at this time of year, so I will make no complaint. I guess it will get to me eventually.

Things are the same as ever here, with nothing to break the monotony. That was one thing about being in combat it never gets at all boring. Something is always happening.

I'm writing this with a bum pen at the Red Cross, so it may not look so wonderful. I guess you will be able to make it out however.

I guess this is all I have to write little though it is. I'll try to write frequently.

Lots of love,

Gene

Mrs E. V. Thurman	Pfc. Earl G. Thurman
304 N. Cheney St.	A.S.N. 34760054
East Point, Ga	Det. Of Patients
	4189 U.S. Army Hospital Plant
	A.P.O. 209 c/o P.M. N.Y. N.Y.

December 12, 1944

Dear Mother,

I was surely glad to receive your two letters today, as it has been several days since I heard from you last. I was also happy to receive my first letter from Nell, too. The news from you two sounds good. I'm glad you're at home now, and feeling alright. Of course I knew you would do too much when you first arrived at home, but I guess that does you less harm than seeing the things go undone! I'm. glad you gave Nell my hospi address, for I would not have heard from her so soon otherwise. I do hope that she can make it home for the Xmas holidays as she plans. I know it will be pleasant for all of you.

I was surprised to know that you entertained the possibility of my being home for Christmas 1944! I guess you are just a typical civilian that doesn't understand the army – and lucky not to, for that understanding is reached only through experience.

Nell seemed to think that you are worried – at least slightly – about my "wound", but I would like to assure you that there is really nothing to worry about. Perhaps you are not so worried since I've been able to write again, but I assure you I'm quite intact. I walked about fifteen miles Sunday PM so I must be!

This is all I have to write now, so I'll "sign off" for a while.

Love to all,

Gene

Miss Nell Thurman
304 N. Cheney St.
East Point, Ga

Pfc. Earl G. Thurman
A.S.N. 34760054
Det. Of Patients
4189 U.S. Army Hospital Plant
A.P.O. 209 c/o P.M. N.Y. N.Y.

December 12, 1944

Dear Nell,

I was certainly glad to hear from you, and mother, today. The news is very encouraging. I think it's fine that you and mother will have a few days together at Christmas. Poor Daddy, he will probably be on a run on Xmas day, as he usually is. Next Christmas maybe we will all be together again for a change.

As for my wounds, there is no need for worry, as I have assured Mother. My hand is doing nicely, as you can see, and I feel fine in general. I'm up and about as good as ever, and have been for several weeks.

I'm sorry I can't be with you, but that shouldn't keep you from having a "Very Merry Christmas"!

Lots of love,
Gene

V-mail, announcing Earl's desire for a woman, with a potential future together, note the improvement in his handwriting:

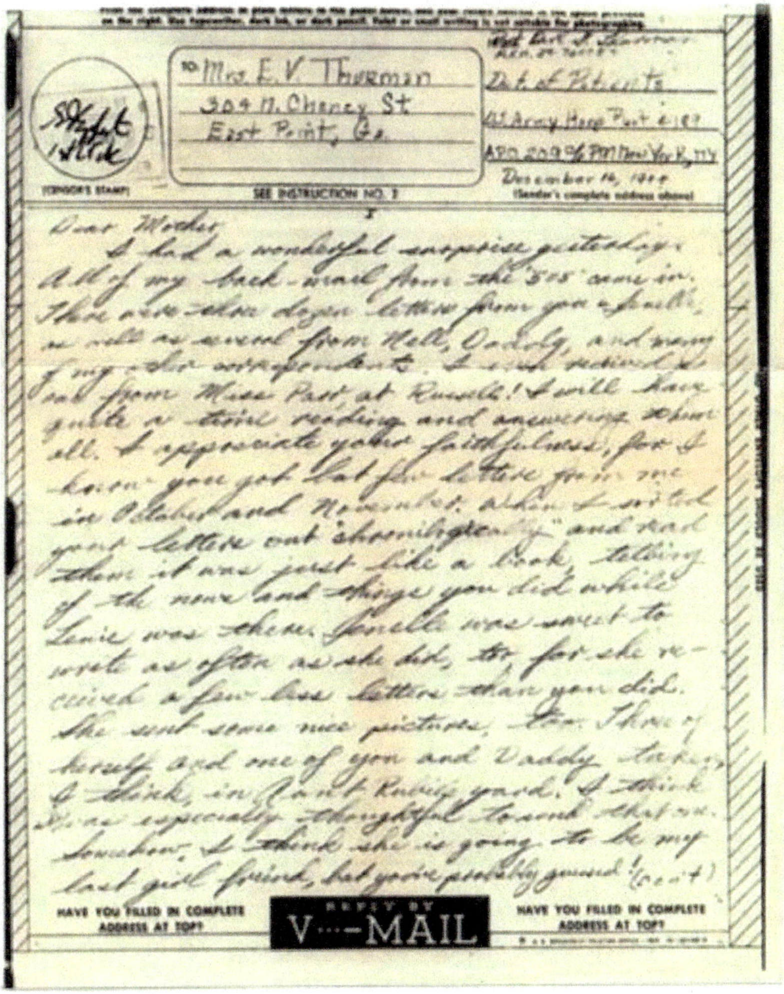

To Mrs. E. V. Thurman
304 N. Cheney St
East Point, Ga.

Det. of Patients
U.S. Army Hosp. Plant 4187
APO 209 c/o PM New York, N.Y.
December 14, 1944
(Sender's complete address above)

CENSOR'S STAMP

SEE INSTRUCTION NO. 2

Dear Mother,

I had a wonderful surprise yesterday. All of my back-mail from the "505" came in. There were three dozen letters from you & Janelle, as well as several from Nell, Daddy, and many of my other correspondents. I even received a card from Miss Pratt at Russell! I will have quite a time reading and answering them all. I appreciate your faithfulness, for I know you got but few letters from me in October and November. When I sorted your letters out "chronologically" and read them it was just like a book, telling of the news and things you did while Lenie was there. Janelle was sweet to write as often as she did, too, for she received a few less letters than you did. She sent some nice pictures, too. Three of herself and one of you and Daddy taken, I think, in Aunt Ruby's yard. I think it was especially thoughtful to send that one. Somehow, I think she is going to be my last girl friend, but you've probably guessed! (con't)

HAVE YOU FILLED IN COMPLETE ADDRESS AT TOP?

REPLY BY V---MAIL

HAVE YOU FILLED IN COMPLETE ADDRESS AT TOP?

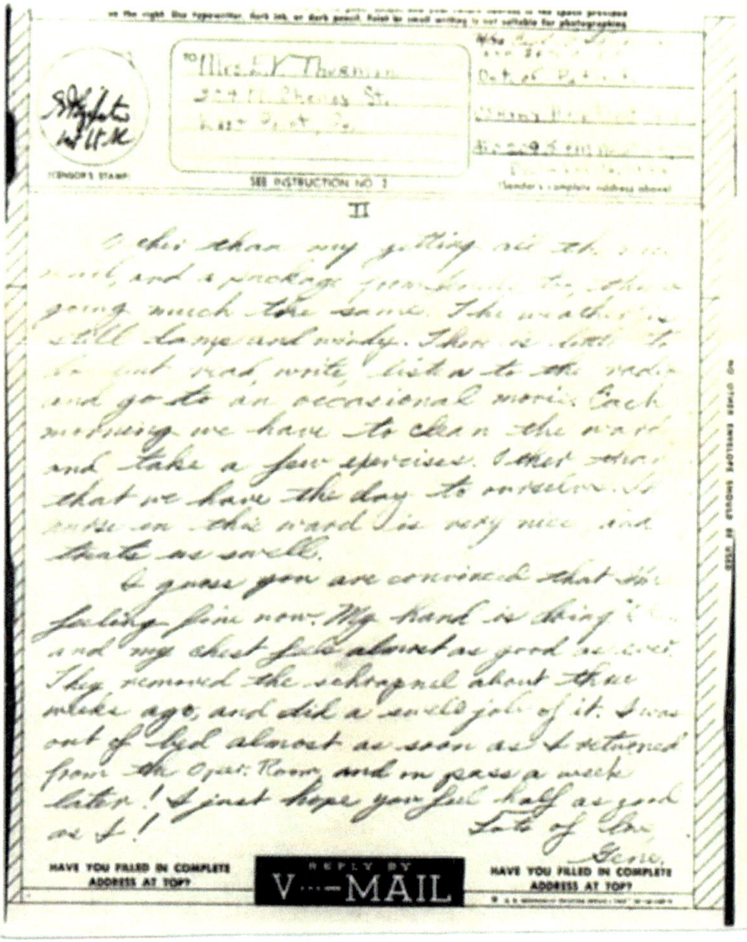

CENSOR'S STAMP

SEE INSTRUCTION NO. 3

(Sender's complete address above)

II

Other than my getting all the [illegible] mail, and a package from home, things are going much the same. The weather is still damp and windy. There is little to do but read, write, listen to the radio and go to an occasional movie. Each morning we have to clean the ward and take a few exercises. Other than that we have the day to ourselves. The nurse on this ward is very nice and thats as swell.

I guess you are convinced that I'm feeling fine now. My hand is doing [illegible] and my chest feels almost as good as ever. They removed the schrapnel about three weeks ago, and did a swell job of it. I was out of bed almost as soon as I returned from the Oper. Room, and on pass a week later! I just hope you feel half as good as I!

Lots of Love
Gene.

HAVE YOU FILLED IN COMPLETE ADDRESS AT TOP?

REPLY BY V---MAIL

HAVE YOU FILLED IN COMPLETE ADDRESS AT TOP?

NO OTHER ENVELOPE SHOULD BE USED

Pfc. Earl G. Thurman
A.S.N. 34760054
Det of Patients
US Army Hospital Plant 4189
A.P.O. 209 c/o P.M. New York N.Y.

Mrs E.V. Thurman
304 N. Cheney St.
East Point, Ga.

December 16, 1944

Dear Mother,

I had a wonderful surprise yesterday all of my back-mail from the "505" came in. There were three dozen letters from you & Jenelle, as well as several from Nell, Daddy, and many of my other correspondents. I even received one from Miss Parr, at Russell! I will have quite a time reading and answering them all. I appreciate your faithfulness, for I know you got back few letters from me in October and November. When I sorted your letters out "chronically" and read them it was just like a book, telling of the news and things you did while Lenie was there. Jenelle was sweet to write as often as she did, too, for she received a few less letters than you did. She sent some nice pictures, too. There of herself and one of you and Daddy taken I think, in Aunt Ruby's yard. I think she was especially thoughtful to send that one. Somehow, I think she is going to be my last girlfriend, but you've probably guessed !

Other than my getting all the new mail, and a package from Jenelle too, things going much the same. The weather is still damp and windy. There is little to do but read, write, listen to the radio and take a few exercises. Other than that we have the day to ourselves. The nurse in this ward is very nice, and treats us well.

I guess you are convinced that I'm feeling fine now. My hand is doing O.K. and my chest feels almost as good as ever. They removed the shrapnel about three weeks ago, and did a swell job of it. I was out of bed almost as soon as I returned from the oper. Room, and on pass a week later! I just hope you feel half as good as I!

Lots of love,

Gene

Pfc. Earl G. Thurman
A.S.N. 34760054
Det of Patients
US Army Hospital Plant 4189
A.P.O. 209 c/o P.M. New York N.Y.

Miss Nell. Thurman
304 N. Cheney St.
East Point, Ga.

December 16, 1944

Dearest Nell,

I had a very pleasant surprise yesterday when I received all of my back-mail. There were fifty or more letters in all, most of which were from you Mother and Jenelle, & I had a lot of fun reading them and I will have quite a bit of writing to do in the next few days before I get up on my writing.

Jenelle sent me some pictures of herself, as well as one of Mother & Daddy together. I thought she was sweet to do that.

Tell Georgia hello for me when you see her. No I certainly haven't forgotten her, she's very nice. I'm happy to hear that things are going so well with you dear, I'm pulling for you. Hope you have a nice time at home.

Lots of love,

Gene

Christmas Day 1944

Pfc. Earl G. Thurman
34760054
Det of Patients
US Army Hospital Plant 4189
A.P.O. 209 c/o P.M. New York N.Y.

Mrs E.V. Thurman
304 N. Cheney St.
East Point, Ga.

December 25, 1944

Dear Mother,

Well, here it is Christmas again! This one is quite different from most of the others, isn't it! I've had a very uneventful day, but last week was a lot of fun for me. I've written you previously about going "Carol singing" two nights in town, which was worlds of fun. Yesterday I went in town to the regular church service, at which we sang more carols. The church people are very hospitable, and I've received several standing invitations to homes. I have also been invited to a party Thursday night. I get along fine in England, don't you think! I hope you, Daddy and Aunt Nina are fine.

Lots of love,

Gene

Mr E.V. Thurman
304 N. Cheney St.
East Point, Ga.

Pfc. Earl G. Thurman
34760054
Det of Patients
US Army Hospital Plant 4189
A.P.O. 209 c/o P.M. New York N.Y.

December 27, 1944

Dear Daddy,
I was very glad to hear from you the other day. I'm always happy to hear that things are going well at home. I hope you have had a pleasant holiday season, with Nell at home. I'm sorry I couldn't be there this year maybe next time I can make it!

Things are going about the same with me, I'm still well and happy at hospital. I guess your read mother's letters in which I mentioned singing Xmas carols. I had a lot of fun last week, but I would enjoy a good old Sacred Harp Singing more than anything else. There will be a time for that too, I guess.

I guess this is all I have just now not that it is news. Hoping you and Mother make out well though the cold weather.

Lots of love,
Gene

Sacred Harp singing is an American tradition of sacred choral music that originated in New England around 1770 and was later carried on in the American South of the United States, especially under the influence of the revival religious services in the 1840's. Its earliest roots are in country parishes of England United Kingdom.
The name derived from the "Sacred Harp," from 1844, a historically important tune book printed in shape notes. The music is performed a cappella, and the singing is participatory rather than a performance to listen to with singers seated by voice in a hollow square. Singings, as Earl refers to them, today are sometimes all-day affairs with shared meals. Shape note singings have crossed back over the Atlantic and today there are singings in Germany, Norway, Ireland, Paris, and Israel.

Pfc. Earl G. Thurman – 34760054
Det. Of Patients U.S.A. Hosp Plant 4189
A.P.O. 209 c/o PM New York, N.Y.

Mrs E.V. Thurman
304 N. Cheney St.
East Point, Ga

December 29th, 1944

Dear Mother,

Here is another little note to let you and the folks know I'm still feeling well, and having a little fun on the side. Just enough fun to keep my morale up, but certainly not too much to keep me from wishing to be home. I guess I will be there in due time.

Last night I went to town again, to a party given by some of the young people at the church. We had a nice time and I felt quite at home after I got acquainted with all the guests. I had wondered how I would find the party but it was about the same as one at home. By this time I have no trouble at all with the English accent, and they seem to have little trouble understanding me. Of course the accents are different, just as at home, according to the section of the country.

I received a V-mail from you dated December 13 yesterday and I was glad to hear that things are still going well with you, Daddy and aunt Nina. I hope they continue the same.

Lots of love,

Gene

1945

American Red Cross letter, January 2nd, 1945, sent to Earl's parents two months after Earl was wounded, hoping that his parents would receive news about his injuries soon:

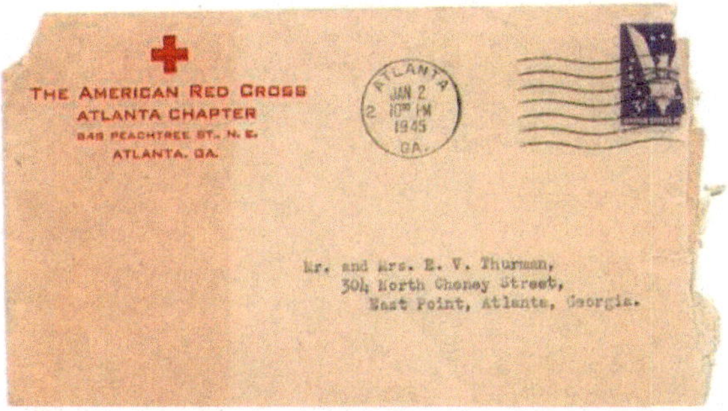
THE AMERICAN RED CROSS
ATLANTA CHAPTER
848 PEACHTREE ST., N. E.
ATLANTA, GA.

ATLANTA
JAN 2
10 PM
1945
GA.

Mr. and Mrs. E. V. Thurman,
304 North Cheney Street,
East Point, Atlanta, Georgia.

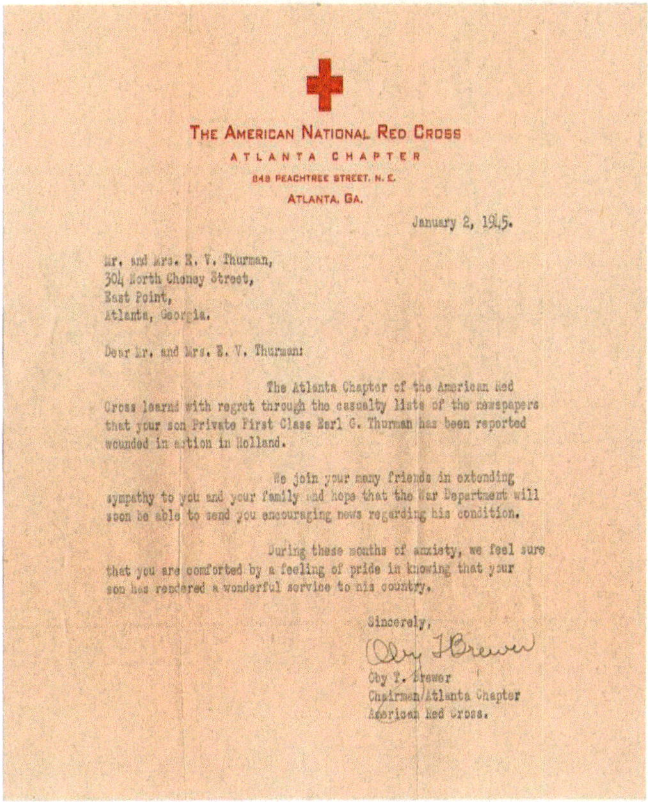
THE AMERICAN NATIONAL RED CROSS
ATLANTA CHAPTER
848 PEACHTREE STREET, N. E.
ATLANTA, GA.

January 2, 1945.

Mr. and Mrs. E. V. Thurman,
304 North Cheney Street,
East Point,
Atlanta, Georgia.

Dear Mr. and Mrs. E. V. Thurman:

The Atlanta Chapter of the American Red Cross learned with regret through the casualty lists of the newspapers that your son Private First Class Earl G. Thurman has been reported wounded in action in Holland.

We join your many friends in extending sympathy to you and your family and hope that the War Department will soon be able to send you encouraging news regarding his condition.

During these months of anxiety, we feel sure that you are comforted by a feeling of pride in knowing that your son has rendered a wonderful service to his country.

Sincerely,

Cby T. Brewer

Cby T. Brewer
Chairman/Atlanta Chapter
American Red Cross.

Between December 21st to 29th 1944 and January 3rd, 1945 Earl wrote on V-mail letters that were sent without being processed, possibly due to lack of writing material. These are splendid examples of the whole-mail process.

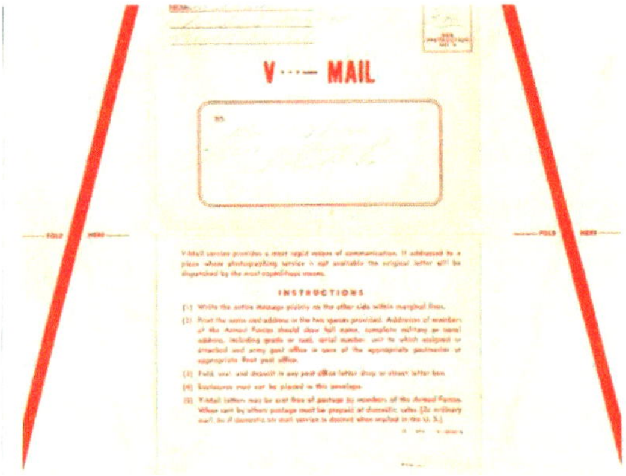

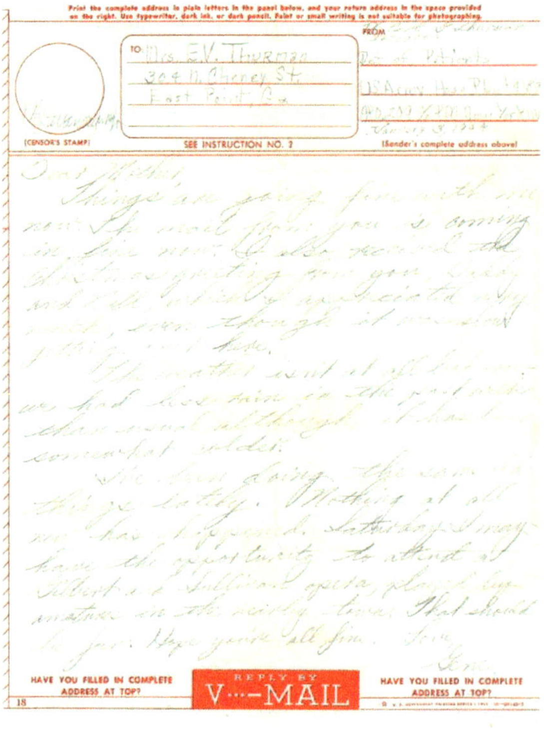

Print the complete address in plain letters in the panel below, and your return address in the space provided on the right. Use typewriter, dark ink, or dark pencil. Faint or small writing is not suitable for photographing.

TO: Mrs. E.V. Thurman
304 N. Cheney St.
East Point, Ga.

FROM: [illegible]
US Army [illegible]
APO [illegible] New York

(CENSOR'S STAMP) SEE INSTRUCTION NO. 2 (Sender's complete address above)

Dear Mother,

Things are going fine with me now. The mail from you is coming in fine now. I also received the Christmas greeting from you, [illegible] and [illegible] [illegible] appreciated very much, even though it [illegible] [illegible] [illegible] here.

The weather isn't at all [illegible] we had [illegible] rain in the past [illegible] [illegible] [illegible] although it has [illegible] somewhat colder.

We [illegible] doing the same things lately. Nothing at all new has happened. Saturday I may have the opportunity to attend a Gilbert and Sullivan opera, played by amateurs in the nearby town. That should be fun. Hope you're all fine. Love,

HAVE YOU FILLED IN COMPLETE ADDRESS AT TOP?

REPLY BY V···—MAIL

HAVE YOU FILLED IN COMPLETE ADDRESS AT TOP?

18

The V-mail would fold into itself to produce the envelope.

How the recipient would receive the photographed copy.

The finished product.

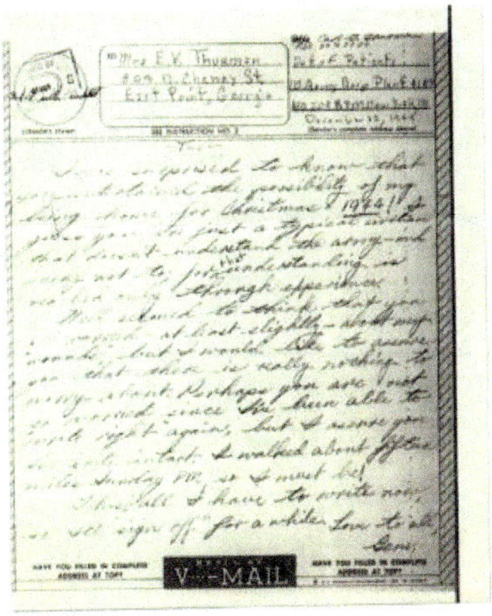

Pvt Earl G. Thurman
34760054
Det of Patients
US Army Hospital Plant 4189
A.P.O. 209 c/o P.M. New York N.Y.

Mrs E.V. Thurman
304 N. Cheney St.
East Point, Ga.

January 3rd, 1945

Dear Mother,

Things are going fine with me now. The mail from you is coming in fine now. I also received the Christmas greeting from you, Daddy and Nell, which I appreciated very much, even though it was slow getting here.

The weather isn't at all bad now we have less rain in the past week than usual although it has been somewhat colder.

I've been doing the same old things lately. Nothing at all new has happened. Saturday I may have the opportunity to attend a Gilbert and Sullivan opera, played by amateurs in the nearby town. That should be fun.

Hope your all fine.

Love,

Gene

Pfc. Earl G. Thurman
34760054
Det of Patients
US Army Hospital Plant 4189
A.P.O. 209 c/o P.M. New York N.Y.

Mrs E.V. Thurman
304 N. Cheney St.
East Point, Ga.

January 6th, 1945

Dear Mother,

I was very glad to receive three of your letters and one from Nell as a birthday present yesterday. The news is good, and the mail took about twelve days.

The weather here is pleasant now although we had a bit of snow yesterday. It didn't stick however. It was nice for Bill to get home at Christmas time. I know all of you, especially his wife, were glad to see him. No doubt he was a big help to his mother around the house.

I'm glad you could have the piano tuned for Nell. I don't know how the pianos she has to use in Chicago are, but I guess she enjoyed playing her own for a change, I would surely like to hear her again myself, I have written Faye since I've been here, although I have received only a Xmas card from her so far. I will possibly hear soon.
I would like to write Julian, but I don't have his address ? I might get to see him if I had it.

I have received no packages this year, but they will probably arrive some day. Some of the packages to other boys are still arriving so mine will come soon I guess. Neither have I gotten the Diary, but I will be glad to receive one.

Tonight, as far as I know now, I'm going in to hear a Gilbert & Sullivan opera called Yeoman of the guard" should be pretty good.

Hope all are fine at home,
Lots of love,
Gene

January 1945.

Pfc. Earl G. Thurman
A.S.N. 34760054
Det of Patients
US Army Hospital Plant 4189
A.P.O. 209 c/o P.M. New York N.Y.

Mrs E.V. Thurman
304 N. Cheney St.
East Point, Ga.

Dear Mother,

I was glad to get your V-mail letter dated Dec 27 last year! The news is good and I'm glad to know that it is such. The gift of orange and tangerine really sounded good to me. I would like to be there and help you eat them.

We have had a bit of snow lately but not enough to stick. I hear that you are having a bit of still weather generally, so I have to be satisfied with the weather we have.

It really isn't so bad. I went to church again yesterday and had to walk about eight miles due to lack of conveyance. It was more fun than anything else to me however I have to walk four miles every night I go to town, so I'm used to it. I received Aunt Nina's Xmas card and appreciated it very much.

Love to all,

Gene

Pfc. Earl G. Thurman
A.S.N. 34760054
Det of Patients
US Army Hospital Plant 4189
A.P.O. 209 c/o P.M. New York N.Y.

Mrs E.V. Thurman
304 N. Cheney St.
East Point, Ga.

January 11. 1945

Dear Mother,

How is everything at home these days. We are having a nice snow today. It is already about two or three inches deep and may get deeper. It isn't so convenient, but it is pretty. From the snow we've had, you may have some snow by now yourself.

Life in the hospital is still a bit boring but I can stand it indefinitely, when I think how cold and miserable it is at the front. This is a comparatively good life, with nice beds and a warm room to stay in.

Your mail is still arriving regularly, as well as that of my other correspondences, none has come today, but it isn't time yet.
I guess this little bit is all I have to say today.

Love to all,

Gene

Pfc. Earl G. Thurman
A.S.N. 34760054
Det of Patients
US Army Hospital Plant 4189
A.P.O. 209 c/o P.M. New York N.Y.

Mrs E.V. Thurman
304 N. Cheney St.
East Point, Ga.

January 15th, 1945

Dear Mother,

Hello again. I hope things are still fine at home. I haven't had a letter in a few days now, but in general the mail system is very good at present. I receive mail from someone almost every day, which is the best mail that has ever come over here.

I've been getting along fine as usual and was in town yesterday for the evening service and the social hour. I enjoyed both the services very much. I always enjoy good music, and they had several good soloists at the "hour". One was a tenor who is a regular member of the church and has a beautiful voice.

I may have a two day pass starting tomorrow. Don't know where I'll go!

Love to all,

Gene

Pfc. Earl G. Thurman
A.S.N. 34760054
Det of Patients
US Army Hospital Plant 4189
A.P.O. 209 c/o P.M. New York N.Y.

Miss Nell Thurman
432 Arlington Pl.
Chicago, Illinois

January 20th, 1945

Dear Nell,

I was very glad to receive your letter telling about your's & Georgia's new apartment. It sounded very nice, and I hope turns out just that way. You really should be over here, Nell. We have a nice blanket of snow over everything. I had a vigorous snow battle last night, I'm still just a little boy you see. It's more fun being that way I guess!

I had a two day pass this week, and I went to Leicester. I had a very nice time but of course two days passes quickly. Tell Georgia that I'll hold her to that promise about a steak if I get back anytime soon.

Lot's of love,
Gene

Pfc. Earl G. Thurman
A.S.N. 34760054
Det of Patients
US Army Hospital Plant 4189
A.P.O. 209 c/o P.M. New York N.Y.

Mrs E.V. Thurman
304 N. Cheney St.
East Point, Ga.

January 22nd, 1945

Dear Mother,

It's a lovely day here, but there is still about four inches of snow. It is melting slowly, but I think it will freeze again tonight. It will certainly, make an awful mess when it melts.

Last night I went in to Church again in town. I spent the afternoon with some of my Church friends, the Davies. They are very nice people and I go in to see them several times a week. It certainly is a relief to get away from the army occasionally.

Today I've been doing my weekly wash and pressing my uniform. Since I've been going out more I've plenty to do.
I hope all is well with you and the rest of the "family".

Lots of love,
Gene

Earl had only been in action for one month when he was seriously wounded on the 17th of October 1944. His wounds were serious enough to have him shipped back to England for an operation to have shrapnel fragments removed that had entered his body from an exploding German 88mm shell. Three months later, his journey would finally be homeward bound.

After the Battle of the Bulge, in the Ardennes Forest, Belgium, during the winter months of December 1944 and January 1945, Hitler's final push to win the war, increased the number of allied casualties in the already over-crowded hospitals, putting a strain on the medical services to return the wounded back to the United States. The U.S. added more transatlantic hospital ships and C-54 transport planes into service to ease the problem.

Movements to return the wounded improved by a vast amount during the tail end of January 1945, with an estimated 24,666 patients returning home to the U.S.A, including Earl.

U.S.A

Postal Stamp: Sent from Boston Mass
Feb 11 9.30pm 1945

From Pfc. Earl G. Thurman – 34760054
Det. Of Patients – Bldg. #7
Halloran Gen Hosp
Staten Island 2, New York

To: Miss Nell Thurman
432 Arlington Place
Chicago, Illinois

Sunday P.M.

February 11, 1945

Dear Nell,

I know Mother will have written you by now, and told you the good news. I'm back in the States and at present am at Lenie's. We got to New York Friday and were given 48 hour passes starting yesterday morning. I caught the twelve o'clock train at Grand Central and am now in good old Boston. I wired Lenie of course, and we killed the fatted calf last night, or at least we got a nice steak from someplace. It is wonderful to have something delicious to eat after being in England for a while. It's almost impossible to get anything good there.

The trip over was slow but, on the whole, pleasant. We were not crowded on the ship, and the food was at least eatable.

I am now stationed at a lovely hospital on Staten Island, New York. I don't know how many days I will be there, but I hope to be sent to a hospital near home and given a furlough in the near future. I'd rather you wouldn't write me at my present address for I probably won't be there long enough to get the letter.

I'm writing the rather hurriedly so you will have to overlook the mistakes. I just wanted you to know "what's what".

Lenie and Judy are both sweeter than ever and ask me to send their love along with mine.

As always,

Gene

Back in America at last, Gene had his first stay at the Halloran General Hospital. Mainly a debarkation hospital for wounded arriving from overseas. The patients were taken to the hospital as soon as they arrived back in the Sates and given preliminary care. After being medically classified they would be sent to other Army hospitals either nearer their homes or specialising in the type of treatment required. "Overnight the hospital may clear out and a whole new batch arrive by the morning. Earl was admitted on the 9th of February 1945.

Postal Stamp: Staten island N.Y. Feb 13 8.30 pm 1945.

Pfc. Earl G Thurman – 34760054
Det. Of Patients Bldg #7
Halloran General Hospital
Staten Island, New York

Mr. E.V. Thurman
304 N. Cheney St
East Point, Ga

Tuesday A.M.

February 13, 1945

Dear Daddy,

Well I hope you are feeling much better today than you were when I phoned Friday night. I'm glad it wont be long now until you can retire and take things easy – and go to every singsong within five hundred miles!

I'm feeling fine now, and have enjoyed myself immensely since I got back to the good old U.S.A. I'm sure you have received the letter I wrote to mother from Boston so I wont have to tell you how much I enjoyed being up to see Lenie & Judy. They both look wonderful, and were just as sweet as ever. I couldn't have been treated any better or made more welcome than I was.

They have a swell apartment, too, just the right size for two people, clean and neat, and just across the street from their work. Of course, it wouldn't do for us!

I left on the twelve P.M. train for New York, but due to some long lay-over or something (I must have been asleep) we didn't get to New York until eight thirty in the morning. I ate and then walked around town looking at the famous sights, such as Times Square, Broadway and the Empire State Building. I went up to the top of the E.S. Building and had a look at the city from above. It was too foggy to see more than the downtown section, including the waterfront where I docked but it was still interesting. I could see the Queen Mary, which came in recently, and many of the famous buildings in town, such as the Chrysler Bldg, Radio City Music Hall, and the R.C.A. building.

By the time I came back down to earth it was almost time to catch my bus, since I had to be back at the hospital at one o' clock. I made it on time with no trouble.

I don't know how the weather is way down South, but its not too good here. We have about given up hope of seeing the ground again, for there is too much snow.

It is snowing more right now, too. Boston was an awful mess. It had started to melt up there.

This is all for now.

Don't write me here, as I'll be moving soon.

Love to all,

Gene

Postal Stamp:
Staten Island N.Y. FEB 15 2PM 1945

Pfc. Earl G. Thurman – 3476054
Det of Patients Bldg #7
Halloran General Hospital
Staten Island, New York

Thursday A.M.

February 15, 1945

Dear Mother,

I didn't think I would be here long enough to write again, but they are keeping me for about a week it seems. I saw my name on a shipping list yesterday and I think I will leave very soon now. I don't know how long I will be held at the next hospital, but I hope it will be long enough to get our clothes cleaned and so forth. After I left Lenie's I went down to New York City for a morning of sightseeing but I told you about that when I wrote to Daddy on Monday.

Actually very little has happened since I came back Monday, I have spent most of my time writing letters to almost all of my correspondents. It is easier to write now that censorship is a thing of the past. We are getting very good food now, but it wont compare with "home-cooking". I hope you are well enough to make me some of those delicious pancakes that you used to make by using left-over bread. That is one thing we never see in the army. We don't get anything but eggs anymore it seems. That is one thing I don't want at home. As you can see, I'm going to be a hard one to please when I get home! That isn't really the truth, though, for just being home will be good enough for me even if I have to live on bread & water!

We still have a bit of snow, but it isn't too cold. I hope the weather is good at home now, for I have seen enough rain & slush for this year. I guess this is about all I have to say for now I hope you and Daddy are feeling fine now and I don't want you to get excited about my coming home and work yourself down. I wont be home for a week or two anyway!

Love to all,

Gene

Postal Stamp:
Fort Benning, GA. 1945 / Jul 13 1130 AM

From: 34760054
Pfc Earl G Thurman
Co "0" 5th Bn. 2nd P.T.R.
Ft. Benning, Ga (A.T.A.)

U.S. ARMY PARACHUTE TROOPS

Mr. E.V. Thurman
304 N. Cheney St.
East Point, Georgia

U.S. ARMY PARACHUTE TROOPS
Wednesday P.M.
July 11, 1945

Dear Daddy,

I hope this letter finds you home, with everything going along smoothly. That is a lot to hope for I realise, but I feel sure that we shall someday have things like that.

I haven't heard from home (even though I've been there, for more than a week,) so I am somewhat in the dark as to the immediate situation. When I was home Mrs Barratt told me of uncle Tom of having another stroke, and that you had gone down for a few days. I presume you put in your share of work while you were there you always do.

I seem to be settled at this address for a while now, and from the looks of things I'm going to like it fine, it's rather hot down here, but we have no drills, no work that is strenuous, and no set uniform. I have plenty of time for almost anything I wish to do so long as I stay around the area of my company. I may not get home again this week-end, but I don't really know yet. There is no need for a long letter, for I can tell you all the little things when I get home.

Once more, I hope you, mother are feeling fine, and not going hungry.

Lots of love,

Gene

Previous letter written on U.S. Parachute Troops headed paper:

U. S. ARMY PARACHUTE TROOPS

Wednesday P.M.
July 11, 1945

Dear Daddy,

I hope this letter finds you home, with everything going along smoothly. That is a lot to hope for I realize, but I feel sure that we shall someday have things like that.

I haven't heard from home (even though I've been there) for more than a week so I am somewhat in the dark as to the immediate situation. When I was home Mrs. Barrett told me of Uncle Love having another stroke, and that you had gone down for a few days. I presume you put in your share of work while you were there – you always do.

U. S. ARMY PARACHUTE TROOPS

I seem to be settled at this address for a while now, and from the looks of things I'm going to like it fine. It's rather hot down here, but we have no drill, no work that is strenuous, and no set uniform. I have plenty of time for almost anything I wish to do, so long as I stay around the area of my company. I may not get home again this week-end, but I don't really know yet.

There is no need for a long letter, for I can tell you all the little things when I get home.

Once more, I hope you & mother are feeling fine, and not going hungry.

Lots of love,

Gene

Pfc. Earl G. Thurman – 34760054
Co "O" 5th Bn. 2nd P.T.R.
Ft. Benning, Ga

Miss Nell Thurman
28 W. 73rd Street
New York 23, N.Y.

Monday P.M.

July 16, 1945

Dear Nell,

I was very glad to receive your letter today. The news is good, and at last we have option of New York city. I don't think any clear thinking, intelligent Indian or tribe would want the place but I believe the Italians and "wholesale" people would pay a reasonable price for it.

I am doing quite well at Benning so far. I have been home for the past two weekends, and have done almost no work between them. I'm now out of the "Alabama Area", back in Georgia at another outpost called "Harmony Church." This is the location of the famous, or infamous, Infantry O.C.S. (Officer Candidate School) and it seems to be cooler and cleaner than the "A.T.A" I also delight in the absence of mosquitos and insects of most all kinds. Of course there is little harmony and as yet I've seen no Church, but there may be one around somewhere.

Last week Wyndal was home, from Germany, and I went out to see him. He hasn't changed one bit, and he looks better than I've ever seen him. He Captured, or rather "liberated", a German camera and somehow got film enough to take dozens of pictures of German wreckage and landscape. He also had some German film which he projected onto a screen. Most of them were scenes of famous Cathedrals and landmarks. We had a great time.

Last night I waited for the Columbia bus in East Point and it finally came by and stopped. Not that it did me any good. He said he was the last bus, but could not take anymore passengers. So there I was I'm glad I didn't lose my right thumb in Holland for it finally got me a ride to Colombia with a couple of officers in a 41 Ford. In the long run I probably beat the bus by half an hour.

The lecture you gave me was very good, and I'm sure you know Mother better than I. I probably have been too "hard" on her about that habit of worrying, but I still think she does, or did too much. I believe she has found it out herself, for she seems much better now.

I'm still terribly dopey from the trip down last night, for I didn't get the first wink of sleep. If this letter seems scribbled and incoherent blame in on that.

I believe I've had my say now. Here's wishing you all the luck and success with your studies and work this summer.

Write if you have time.

Worlds of love,

Gene

Postal Stamp:
Fort Benning G.A. 1945 SEP 6 4-PM

Pfc Earl G Thurman – 34760054
Co, "O" 5th Bn. 2nd P.T.R.
Ft Benning, Georgia

Mr. E. V. Thurman
304 N. Cheney St
East Point, Ga

Thursday a.m. September 6, 1945

Dear Daddy

Well guess what has happened to your little boy! They've put him in the hospital, believe it or not! That cold kept giving me trouble, so I walked over and saw the "Medic" about it yesterday. They found that I had a temperature (100.2) and sent me right over here to the hospital on the main post. The doctor in my ward says I'll be alright after a day or two in bed. I only had a headache yesterday, but that is gone now, and also the aching in and around my eyes. I doubt if I get away from the hospital before Saturday or Sunday, as they usually keep you in for two or three days after you're well. Just to be sure, partly, and then there is always plenty of red tape involved.

It is a nice sunny day, but not nearly as hot as it has been lately. I think the bad weather is about gone for good. Oops, I mean for winter. It'll be here again next year.

This seems to be about all I can think of now.

Much love to you and Mother,

From Gene

Postal Stamp:
Fort Benning G.A. 1945 SEP 19 9.30AM

Pfc Earl G Thurman – 34760054
Co, "O" 5th Bn. 2nd P.T.R.
Ft Benning, Georgia

Mrs. E. V. Thurman
304 N. Cheney St
East Point, Ga

Monday P.M. September 17th, 1945

Dear Mother,

Here's a little note to let you know that I had a nice trip down yesterday, and I'm now out of the main hospital and down at "Harmony church area at the "reconditioning" center.

I shouldn't be here, but a new order stating that everyone comes here when they leave the hospital, is responsible. I really don't mind, for we have sheets and good food and I certainly didn't have any such luxuries as that in Alabama. I will be here for a week or two and then go back to duty in Alabama. I probably will not be able to get home for a week or two now. The weather is not at all bad, but it is still just the least bit too warm. Tonight I went over to a show and saw a picture called "Captain Kidd," with Charles Laughton, which was rather good.

I hope you are a lot easier today, and be sure to take care of yourself and Daddy.

Much love,

Gene

SEARCHING FOR EARL

Searching for Earl was a necessity to complete his life story, as well as finding out about his family. His father, Earl Senior, married twice. His first wife, Willa Cox, died after they were married for only six years. During the brief time they were together, they had a son, Cyril, born on the 24th of November 1908. Unfortunately, he would also lose his life at the youthful age of 13. In 1916, Earl Senior would re-marry Launette Glass, and the ceremony would be carried out by her brother, Reverend Lemuel Page. A year later, Launette would give birth to their daughter Nell. Seven years later, Earl Junior would be born.

Earl Senior passed away at the age of 79, thirty-seven days after Launette passed away, aged 75.

Nell Thurman, at the age of 35 married Paul Engelstad in 1952. They divorced, on the 2nd of July 1981, Nell passed away at the grand old age of 102.

In a letter dated 16th December, Earl Junior wrote,

"Jenelle was sweet to write as often as she did, too, for she received a few less letters than you did. She sent some nice pictures, too. There of herself and one of you and Daddy taken I think, in Aunt Ruby's yard. I think she was especially thoughtful to send that one. Somehow, I think she is going to be my last girlfriend, but you've probably guessed!"

Unfortunately, I was unable to find any records of Jenelle, so whether they dated after his return home from the battlefront I was not able to conclude the fact. I did, however, trace that the whole family moved to Texas in the mid-1950s.

As the search continued the smallest piece of information in one of Earl's letters gave a clue about his past before enlisting in the army. The letter dated 16th December 1944 mentioned Miss Parr from Russell.

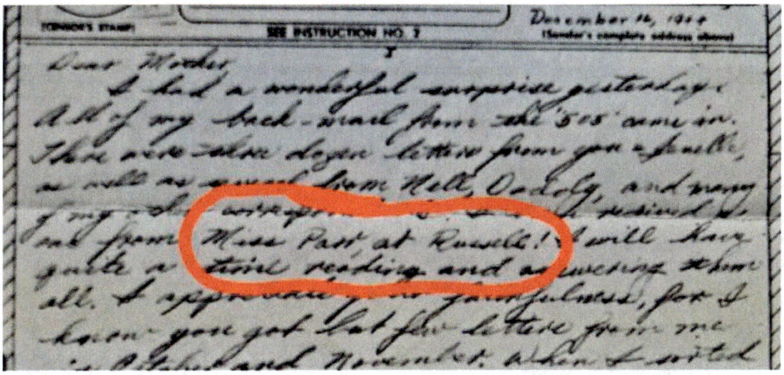

December 16, 1944
(Sender's complete address above)
SEE INSTRUCTION NO. 2

Dear Mother,
I had a wonderful surprise yesterday.
All of my back-mail from the 505 came in.
There were three dozen letters from you & family,
as well as several from Nell, Dorothy, and many
of my [illegible] I received
one from Miss Parr at Russell! I will have
quite a time reading and answering them
all. I appreciate [illegible] faithfulness, for I
know you got but few letters from me
in October and November. When I wrote

A quick search on the web, led me to hunch that Earl studied at the Russell High School in his hometown and Miss Parr may have been a teacher. With this information I second guessed a period of when Earl may have attended the school searching an on-line auction site for old yearbooks from the Russell high school. I sent three different seller's messages enquiring about Miss Parr and Earl, you can imagine my delight when one replied saying there was a photograph of Miss Parr in the 1940 yearbook, I purchased a copy from Dave Nelson from Kennesaw, Georgia. Dave took an interest in my project and promptly started to help me research from America. With the help of Dave and Gary Pinkerton from the Texas Historical Association the book's conclusion came together.

Class Photo of Earl taken in 1938 from the
Russell High School yearbook

Second row from the top, from left to right Earl is smartly dressed in the fifth position.

Earl as a University Student at the Emory University 1951, third from the left.

Original copy of Pointer the Russell High School as 1940 Yearbook purchased from Dave Nelson which revealed Miss Parr.

Miss Louis Parr, Earls teacher.

Advisor Miss Lois Parr

Russell
HONOR SOCIETY

Nell Thurman Russell High School 1935 Earl's older sister.

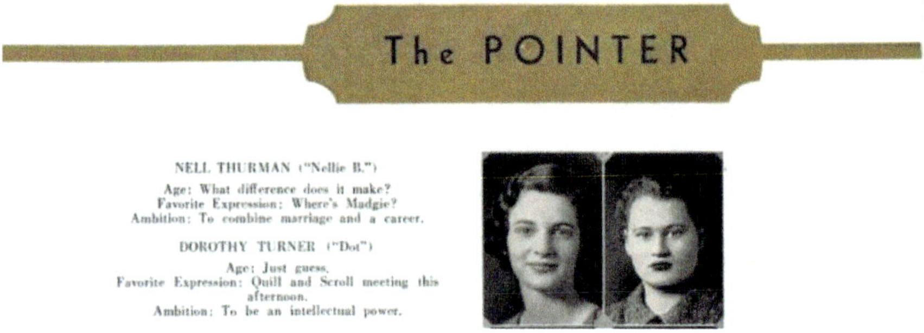
The POINTER

NELL THURMAN ("Nellie B.")

Age: What difference does it make?
Favorite Expression: Where's Madgie?
Ambition: To combine marriage and a career.

DOROTHY TURNER ("Dot")

Age: Just guess.
Favorite Expression: Quill and Scroll meeting this afternoon.
Ambition: To be an intellectual power.

Newspaper clippings from the collection featuring a picture of the Honourable Discharge Emblem, a patch worn on uniforms after being discharged from service. Referred to as the "ruptured duck" because it was thought the eagle looked more like a duck in poor shape.

Tragically, Earl G. Thurman's life was taken away from him while in his prime at the age of 33. A graduate of Emory University, he moved to Texas with his mother and father where he was employed at the Tyler (Texas) Junior college as a professor of language. Earl was visiting Mexico City to improve his knowledge of Spanish when it was reported in a local newspaper that he had been brutally attacked. He was found beaten and left in a coma from which he did not recover.

His attackers had stripped him of identification, money, and belongings in the suburb of San Angel on August 14th, 1957. He passed away three days later. Two Mexican bricklayers, Silvano Martinez and Lorenzo Espinosa, were identified as his murderers. No records show if these men were ever brought to justice.

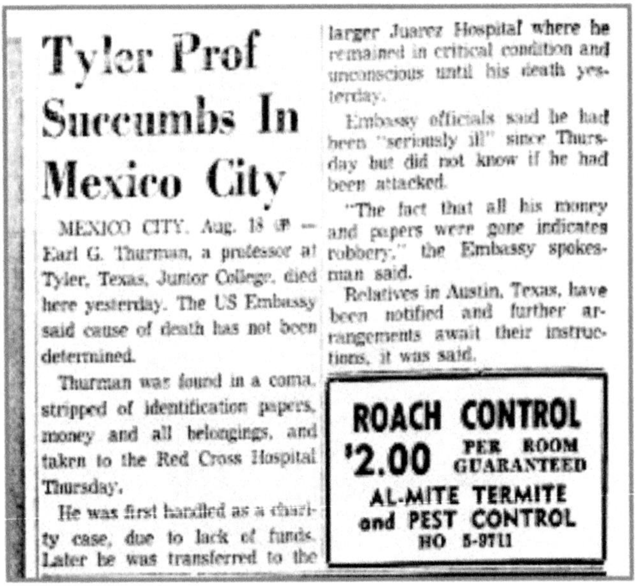

Tyler Prof Succumbs In Mexico City

MEXICO CITY, Aug. 18 (AP) — Earl G. Thurman, a professor at Tyler, Texas, Junior College, died here yesterday. The US Embassy said cause of death has not been determined.

Thurman was found in a coma, stripped of identification papers, money and all belongings, and taken to the Red Cross Hospital Thursday.

He was first handled as a charity case, due to lack of funds. Later he was transferred to the larger Juarez Hospital where he remained in critical condition and unconscious until his death yesterday.

Embassy officials said he had been "seriously ill" since Thursday but did not know if he had been attacked.

"The fact that all his money and papers were gone indicates robbery," the Embassy spokesman said.

Relatives in Austin, Texas, have been notified and further arrangements await their instructions, it was said.

The Austin American Mon Aug 19, 1957.

Tyler Morning Telegraph

Probers Won't Hear BenJack

Ike, Dulles Study Syrian Crisis

Attorney Promises His Return

Autopsy Shows Tyler Teacher Victim Of Fatal Blow On Head

Ike Doctrine Blamed For Syrian Troubles

Guide For Small City Financial Aid Adopted

CAMP FORD SITE OF CONFEDERATE PRISON

"Autopsy Shows Tyler Teacher Victim of Fatal Blow On Head"

Tyler Morning Telegraph Tue Aug 20, 1957.

El Paso Times Tue Aug 20, 1957.

Blow On Head Cited As Cause Of Prof's Death

Mexico City. (AP) — A Tyler junior college professor, found dying on the streets of a suburb here last Wednesday had been fatally struck on the head, an autopsy report said Monday.

The professor, Earl G. Thurman, who gave an Austin address, died Friday after apparently being on the road to recovery.

A check of hotels showed that he checked into Hotel Hunter Aug. 10, and checked out Aug. 12, saying he was making a trip to Oaxaca, about 350 miles southeast of Mexico City, and would return in a day or two.

The Red Cross said he was picked up in a coma about 7 a. m. Wednesday in the Mexico City suburb of San Angel.

Still unknown is the location of Thurman's baggage and what he did from Monday until Wednesday.

Body of Texan Due Return From Mexico Friday

MEXICO CITY, Aug. 22 (AP) — The body of Earl G. Thurman, [illegible] a Texas professor [illegible] killed here last week, will be sent back to Texas Friday.

Thurman, a professor at Tyler Junior College, was traveling here when he died.

An autopsy report said he died of a skull fracture but a [illegible] report was contradictory. It said he died of a form of intoxication from an unknown substance, and that there were no external injuries. The report conflicts with doctor's statements.

Thurman was in Mexico on a vacation. On Aug. 12 he checked out of the Hunter Hotel here saying he was going to [illegible]. Whether he got there is not known.

He was found unconscious in a suburb last Wednesday, stripped of money and belongings.

Fort Worth Star Mon Thur 22, 1957.

Wichita Falls Record News
Aug 22,1957.

Body Will Be Returned

MEXICO CITY, Aug. 22 (AP)—The body of a Texas professor killed here last week will be returned home Friday.

The [illegible] Funeral [illegible] said the body of Karl G. Thurman, 33, of Tyler Junior College, will be sent by train to the [illegible] Funeral Home, Laredo, where relatives from Austin will claim it.

Meanwhile, how the traveling Texan met death remains a mystery although an autopsy report said he died of a skull fracture.

A [illegible] report today was contradictory. It said he died of a form of [illegible] from an unknown [illegible] and that there were no external injuries. This conflicts with [illegible] reports.

Thurman came to Mexico [illegible] and on Aug. 12 checked out of the [illegible] Hotel here saying he was going to Oaxaca. Whether or not he ever got to Oaxaca is not known.

Thurman, stripped of money and of belongings, was found unconscious in a suburb of Mexico City last Wednesday and taken to a Red Cross hospital. Later he was moved to [illegible] hospital, where he died Saturday.

Officials said Thurman may have been hit by a car, but the fact he was stripped of money and belongings indicated he had been slugged and robbed.

[illegible] course.

Police Identify Texan's Slayers

MEXICO CITY, Aug. 25 (AP)—Police identified Sunday two Mexican bricklayers as the attackers of Karl G. Thurman of Tyler, Texas, junior college professor who died Aug. 17 from a blow on the head.

Thurman, 33, was found slugged and robbed in the suburb of San Angel early Aug. 14. He died three days later in a hospital.

Police said the bricklayers, Silvano Martinez and Lorenzo Espinosa Hernandez, were questioned Aug. 16 after a policeman reported the two struck a man on the head with a shovel in the San Angel section. They were released at the time, investigators said, because the victim could not be found.

Police Commander Aguilar Santaolalla said he expects to arrest the two men soon.

Fort Worth Star
Aug 26, 1957.

Earl as a professor of language at the Tyler Junior college Texas 1957.

Left to right, family portrait:

Earl Gene Thurman - Launette Glass Thurman
Nell Thurman Engelstad.

Daddy - Earl Vandorn Thurman October 4th, 1880, February 14th, 1960

Mother - Launette Glass Thurman August 18th, 1880, January 9th, 1960

Nell Thurman Engelstad June 16th, 1917 – July 2nd, 2019

Pictured below, Nell Thurman Engelstad, a retired music and piano teacher, passed away July 2nd, 2019, aged 102.

Her Obituary read:
She did her best under difficult circumstances as a single parent.

Earl Gene Thurman
January 5th, 1924, August 18th, 1957
Aged 33

May he Rest in Peace.

Printed in Great Britain
by Amazon

42617249R00076